# Finding Manna

Debra J K Bronkema

# Parson's Porch Books

www.parsonsporchbooks.com


*Finding Manna*
ISBN: Softcover 978-0-692-30872-1
Copyright © 2018 by Debra J K Bronkema

# Dedication

Finding Manna is dedicated to

My husband John
My children Cali, Dylan, Logan and Caleb,
My parents Ronald and Marilyn Kevern

with much gratitude for their love and support.

# Prologue

There were more words coming out of his mouth. She knew that because his lips were still moving. But all she could hear, over and over again in her head was, "You're not the one."

His beautiful eyes - she suddenly noticed they had gone cold. Clare memorized everything about his face, while the words kept coming at her. She stayed paralyzed in her chair - and when he put his hand on the doorknob, she almost just let him walk away. But then she heard herself speak.

"Danny?" He turned fully toward her, though it was obvious what he really wanted was to run.

"You just figured this out now? A week before graduation?"

He looked to one side - then nodded.

She wanted to scream, cry, hit him with all she had in her. Then the flowers he'd given her caught her eye. She picked them up out of the vase - and hurled them at him with all her strength. Roses and water covered him briefly before they fell to the floor.

Danny's face froze, stunned at her lack of calm acceptance of his words. He turned the knob and walked, well kind of ran, out of her life.

"Okay," Clare said, looking around the room that felt completely empty. "What do I do now?"

# Chapter 1

It was the voice in her head that did it. Without the voice, her bedroom in Michigan with the high school posters on her wall would probably still be her home. But going to live with her parents after she finished school had never been Clare's plan. And no matter how scary it was to move by herself, she really didn't want her life to go backwards.

So, when she woke up a week after graduation with this strong voice in her head saying, 'If a new life is what you're after - why not start over in paradise?' she got on-line and made a plan. Now, six months and twelve days as a resident of Florida – and if somebody asked where she was from, she'd still say Michigan. It wasn't that she regretted her move south. After all, how could she regret moving to a place where the view outside her window was palm trees and perpetual sunshine? What more could anybody want?

Still, taking a risk and moving to Florida on her own, without a job, qualified as the most adventurous thing Clare had ever done. She found a decent job as an accountant right away, which gave her family something to be proud about, instead of just worried. They pretended to think it was great that she was living life in everybody else's idea of a dream vacation. But Clare knew that her parents and her younger sister Kate were spending half their time worrying about her.

As if on cue - Kate called.

"Hey, Kate, What are you doing up so early? I thought law students slept 'til 11."

"Yeah! Right. Actually, I haven't been to bed yet. I wanted to find out what happened with the guy you met in the grocery store. The lunch date guy?"

"Oh…him. Turns out, I misread the signs. I thought buying that many groceries meant he was local. But in reality, he and his buddies were just here for a long weekend – guess they like to eat a lot. Lunch was fine, but that was the end of the story."

"That's a bummer."

"It's okay. I just don't think it's worth talking to people anymore. As far as I can tell, they're all on their way back up north."

"Come on Clare. I looked it up. 50,000 people live in Sarasota. What about at work?"

"Don't most people think dating people you work with is a bad idea? Plus, they're all accountants – not such scintillating conversationalists if you know what I mean."

"Um – Sis – I hate to break this to you - but you're an accountant too. You chose it just like them." As soon as Kate said it, Clare could tell she wanted to take it back. They both knew she'd spent three years with Danny encouraging her to get a job to make money, so he could pursue his music. She had gone on with her master's in accounting while he spent a fifth year finishing his music degree, to stay in school with him, and give herself the best chance to make enough money for both of them. Clare was good at what she did, but they both knew where her career path really came from.

Trying to keep her tone light, Clare said, "So, on that note... I think I'll hang up. Got to get to work - new client today."

"I'm sorry, I shouldn't have said that. I was trying to tease you into giving your coworkers a shot. Too soon, huh?"

"Yup - too soon. It's okay Kate – I'll talk to you later."

Too soon. When wouldn't it be too soon to be reminded of Danny? Clare was pretty sure it would always be too soon.

# Chapter 2

Pulling up to Shepherd's Center, Clare started thinking about what her supervisor Pete had told her about this client. 'It's a counseling center. They've been in operation for almost a year, and they've just come to the conclusion that they should have put an accounting system in place. It's a mess. They need somebody to come in, see what they've done, and then fix it. It's all yours Clare. You're the best fixer I've got.'

Being good at her job was - well better than not being good at it. But it also meant she got more than her fair share of difficult cases. She was on the road a lot, which was interesting - but also kind of lonely. Short-term relationships with strangers weren't really helping her make friends to fill her too long weekends.

Walking into the empty reception area, Clare was struck by how the room gave off an air of peacefulness. The gifts people had that she didn't - gifts like interior decorating that could actually produce a feeling in another person.

Gifts people have that she didn't - like playing the piano. Suddenly Clare felt as if she'd been punched in the stomach. She could see Danny in her mind – making music in a way that made every song his own. Taking a deep breath, she looked around the room. Just then a woman came from the back. "Hi, I'm Susan Manley, the office administrator. Are you from Lincoln and Moss?"

"Yes, I'm Clare Wheeler." Clare was always relieved when people picked her out as an accountant. Whenever she went on the road, she was careful to wear her long blonde hair pulled back, and dress in one of her grey suits matched with low heels. Gaining people's confidence was a lot easier if she didn't have to overcome looking too young to be a professional.

"Oh, Thank Goodness!  Boy do we need you."

"Well then, I'm glad to be here."

"You say that now. Wait until you see the mess I've made of the books. Although I have to tell you it's not all my fault. One of the Board members thought we'd save money by designing our own accounting software." Susan rolled her eyes.

Clare smiled, "I'm sure I've seen worse."

"Oh, don't be so sure. I think it's best if you have very low expectations. I should have spoken up. It's just that I love this job so much, and I didn't want to make anybody angry. Let me finish getting that list you sent to me on Friday together - I'll be right back."

Sitting and waiting, Clare noticed the music playing softly in the background - very peaceful. She let it take her back in time to a memory.

*"The bottom line is my band has this awesome shot! I booked a recording studio with a guy that was at the club last weekend - way under market price." Danny's smile and his excitement were both contagious.*

*"That's incredible!" Clare was almost as excited as he was.*

*"I know right?" He pauses, and she feels the change in his body language before he speaks the next words. "There is one thing."*

*"What is it?" Clare asks. She knows - of course she knows.*

*"$1000. We need that to pay the guy, and none of us have it."*

*"I have it." She said, simply.*

*"Really?"*

*"I saved it over the summer." Clare had waitressed at the Cheesecake Factory at night since her internship at General Motors was only 9-5. She didn't hesitate. For such a time as this. That's what the money was all about. She worked to support his gift. They were a team.*

"Clare?" Susan's voice called her back from the past, to the now. This place, where she made money that no longer had any hope of making music come to life.

Clare very purposefully dug into the records as if she was working on a jigsaw puzzle. She spread everything out all over the room, and began to make piles, finding organization and patterns out of what was chaos. The time went so fast she jumped when Susan came to the door.

"I'm just letting you know that I need to leave now. If you want to keep working the center will be open late tonight; you can just close the door of this room when you leave, and everything will be right where you left it in the morning."

Clare never stayed when the office staff left, because it made them nervous, even if they said it didn't. On the way to her car, she heard her phone signal social media alerts and looked down as a reflex action. Her co-workers didn't seem to be having any trouble finding exciting ways to spend their off-hours. Not that they hadn't invited her to come out with them when she first got the job. And Clare had tried going out on a few Friday nights when she first got to the firm, hoping to connect with people - but drinking too much and hooking up with a stranger, or almost stranger - just wasn't her thing. Never was actually. She'd always been more of a long-term person. Make friends - get to know friends better - date friends. That was her pattern. The bars her co-workers went to were so noisy - she didn't feel like she'd ever get to know people that way.

But that didn't mean she wasn't jealous of the smiles on their faces in all the pictures. Clare wanted to feel the way they looked. Not ready to go home to her empty apartment quite yet, she decided to explore the neighborhood around the counseling center.

Right next-door was a church. Curious, Clare tried the door, and was kind of surprised it was unlocked. There was a sign that said Worship Sundays at 10 A.M. and 5 P.M., but no other hours listed, and no one seemed to be around. Clare wandered through the halls and found the sanctuary. It was in the shape of an octagon, huge, light and sunny – there were windows everywhere. Up north churches usually had stained glass, but this place must have decided that looking out on the blue Florida sky was beautiful enough.

Growing up Clare's family was an every Sunday in church family. To the point that when their car broke down one Saturday night, her Dad woke them early and told them to put on their sneakers, because they'd be walking the mile to church.

That's what church was to Clare. Something you did with your family, to start the week off right. Part of her childhood experience. But going to church on her own had never been something Clare could imagine doing. Whenever her Mom caught on that Clare was lonely, she'd say, "Why don't you try finding a church to make friends?" That might have worked for Clare's parents - they were already a couple when they moved to her hometown. She recognized that going to church alone might be socially acceptable in theory; she just couldn't picture herself doing it. Plus, it was a different time. Her guess was that people didn't spend so much time partying on Saturday nights back then. She was willing to bet nobody her age got up on Sunday mornings before noon unless they were going to work.

Still there was something about this place. She ran her hands over the wood of the pews and walked closer to the art on the walls - abstract fabric made to look like flames and flowers and water. The whole place seemed alive, which was a strange word to come to her mind, with no sign of life in the building. She could just feel it in the air.

On the way out, a poster caught Clare's eye: *Volunteer Help Wanted* in large colorful print. Underneath the title, the sign said, "If you love meeting new people, and know your way around the kitchen, Manna House feeding program is looking for you!"

Manna House. Wasn't there a story in the Bible about manna? Something about God providing food for hungry people? Clare surprised herself by ripping a little slip with the contact information off the bottom of the poster, wondering whether she'd ever have the nerve to follow up.

# Chapter 3

Back home, the piece of paper with the Manna House number on it wouldn't leave her alone. She began to clean up her apartment, straightening the papers on her dining room table and cleaning the kitchen counters, but the nagging of the paper in her purse forced her to pull it out and look at it again. Trying to convince herself that it was too late in the day to call, Clare was about to put it on the bulletin board next to the refrigerator. She was almost pinning it in, when the little voice in her head said, "If you do that, you'll never call."

So, she picked up the phone, dialed – and somebody answered!

"Hello, you've reached Manna House. Can I help you?"

"Well actually, I guess I'm calling to find out if I can help you. I saw your sign at…" Clare's mind suddenly went blank - she couldn't remember the name of the church she'd been at.

Clare's pause went on long enough that the woman rescued her. "Was it at a church maybe?"

"Yes – the one over on Bee Ridge."

"Great! We are advertising for volunteer help. We need people who can commit to working every week, one night a week. Somebody who will make sure things go smoothly for the volunteers and our guests."

Wow. Every week. How could she do that? With tax season and everything?

On the other hand, her firm did give a night off a week even during tax season. And – the rest of the year – let's face it – her social life wouldn't interfere.

Clare heard herself saying yes, before any more reasons to say no came to mind.

"Great! We're running a training this coming weekend. You can come check it out, and then if everything seems right to you and to our trainer, we'll put you on the schedule." No slow-moving process apparently. Come to think of it, whenever Clare listened to that voice in her head, she ended up jumping into things up to her eyeballs.

The next call she made was to Kate. She answered on the first ring.

"Hey sis – what's up?"

"Well – the voice that told me to move to Florida just told me to call and volunteer for something."

"And did you?"

"Yes."

"Clare – seriously? The deal was that you call me and then you choose to follow the voice's advice." Kate only sounded as if she was half joking. She was eleven months younger than Clare, but at this moment she had obviously decided to play the role of big sister.

"You know I'm not crazy right?"

"I know you're not crazy. But when people talk about voices in their heads…"

"It's a good voice, Kate. A strong voice. A voice that wants me to be brave."

"I'm all for brave, Clare. Totally in favor of brave. Just wanting you to maybe do a little analyzing, a little reflecting, before you get up and move a plane ride away." Her voice rose at the end of the sentence, which made Clare smile.

"Well this time, I'm not moving anywhere. I'm just doing something new, and I think that could be a good thing for me. And hopefully for the people I volunteer to help."

"Okay – I can't be against that I guess."

"No, no you really can't. So how are things with you?"

"Well… my professor for contracts is acting like he thinks sleep is a luxury. The reading's okay when it's interesting but trying to keep my eyes open at 4 in the morning on the boring parts – doesn't actually work."

"See this is why volunteering sounds nuts to you – because you don't have time. But I do."

"Really?"

"I really do. And I want to do it – so tell me the voice in my head was brave, not crazy – okay?"

"Okay. Go fix the world's problems sister."

"Love you."

"Love you too."

# Chapter 4

The rest of the week – Clare kept thinking about the leap she was taking. Luckily, she had the puzzle that was Shepherd's Counseling Center to keep her occupied.

Susan came into the room with a coffee that smelled amazing.

"I thought I'd bring you something to keep you awake. Kind of a peace offering?"

"Thank you - you didn't have to do that. But I'm glad you did! What's that smell? It doesn't seem like regular coffee."

"I add some cinnamon to the blend. For some reason cinnamon always makes me smile." Susan said, clearly pleased that Clare had noticed.

"Well, thanks - I'm getting pretty far here today, so I'll probably be ready with some questions early next week."

"I'll do my best to answer them!" said Susan.

As Clare worked through the Shepherd's Counseling records, finding the answers she needed, she still had this nervousness in her stomach that wouldn't really let her go. Eventually she decided she just wanted Saturday to be there, so she'd know for sure what she'd gotten herself into.

The training was happening at what looked, according to the website, to be a large Presbyterian Church, which was definitely within her comfort zone. Growing up Clare's friends were always jealous of all the kids from other grades and even other towns she knew, because of church. Kate once described church as helping them color outside the lines of the social pecking order of their school. Recognizing that at this point, Clare felt like she had no idea how to color inside or outside the lines, she tried to have hope that this move she'd made would actually help.

Clare woke up early on Saturday and got to the building a few minutes before 9:00 in case finding the room was tricky, and that was a good move, because the building was huge. Luckily, she found a sign that led her to a room they probably used for children, judging by the smallish chairs around the tables.

The "crowd" of volunteers Clare had been expecting turned out to be her and one other woman who appeared to be about 60. The leader in the front of the room looked like she'd be spending the day with the two of them, judging by all the material she had in front of her.

"Good morning. I'm Pam Smith, and I'm a member of the Manna House Board, here to orient you this morning. I'm glad to see the two of you. Although we'd always love more people to get involved we happen right now to have need of two hospitality leaders to cover two nights – so, as you can see – two is the perfect number this morning." She smiled as if what she'd said was comforting – and maybe it was to her. To Clare, it meant she better learn all she could, because she was about to be thrown into the deep end.

"Why don't we start by saying our names, and whether you've ever worked with homeless people before."

"I'm Clare Wheeler, and no, I've never done anything like this before."

"I'm Lisa Jordan, and this is new for me too."

Pam said. "That's fine. No prior experience necessary."

"So, for starters, one thing that might surprise you is that you'll find that many of our guests are not that different from you. They've just gone through a hard time and lost the ability to make their way."

"Some were just making it before the housing bubble burst. They lost their jobs, and eventually their homes, and once you're in this cycle, it's pretty tough to get it back together again. And then there are the people who came here as immigrants, and aren't making enough to live on, so they need the food we can provide. Some had a bad accident that ate up all their money and left them on the streets. And some people have addiction issues, or mental health issues."

She went on, "The technical part of this job is easy. I could write it to you in a one-page e-mail, and you'd have it down. It's the people part that we're looking for – somebody who can both manage lots of well-meaning people and be a presence for our guests. Oh, that's what we call the people who eat here. It helps us remember that that's how we want to treat them, as guests in our home."

Pam went on, "We believe in having rules that make sense, and creating an atmosphere of consistency – so that no matter when you come here, you know what to expect. You might think that sounds rigid, but you've got to think about how chaotic many of these people's lives are from sun-up to sundown. They appreciate having Manna House as a rock they can count on."

"And you're looking for us to be part of the rock?" Lisa asked.

"Exactly. We think if we have hosts they can count on, people they recognize, they might find this place to be more of a support, maybe even a place they can connect with, on their way to living off the streets."

"Our volunteers come from a variety of religious groups, some school groups and some community organizations. Sometimes they'll know each other, sometimes they won't. Sometimes they'll have been to Manna House before; sometimes they will be brand new. One of your challenges will be to get them quickly oriented and ready to go by the time you open the doors at 6 p.m. on the dot. No guests can be in the building before the doors open. People line up single-file to get their first helping, served buffet style by the volunteers. Seconds are served family-style - the volunteers divide up what's left into bowls or pans and each table can come up and get seconds."

"Once volunteers are done serving, they sit with the guests, sharing a meal with them. Volunteers should not sit at a table by themselves. Making sure this happens will be another challenge, because you'll notice some of the volunteers are shy. They'll need you to help pave the way for them to sit down with strangers."

Then she paused and said "Now, there's one more thing, and I saved it for last because I want to emphasize just how important this is. If you remember nothing else I've told you, remember this." She didn't even have to say that last part out loud. They could hear it in her tone of voice and see it in the ways her eyes flashed.

"Never, ever ask people to tell you how they ended up on the streets. It is their story. It belongs to them. You don't have a right to know, and if you ask, they'll feel as though they have to tell you in order to get fed."

Clare could see how that would be wrong, but she also knew herself well enough to know that she'd be curious. "What if they start talking about it?"

"That's different. Totally different. Like I said, it's their story. If they want to tell it, I hope you'll listen as attentively as you possibly can. And I hope you'll find a way not to be judgmental toward them, no matter what they tell you."

Lisa spoke up, "Even if they talk about drugs?"

"Even then. Just listen to their story and show whatever empathy you can. Now, if someone is obviously actively using when they come into Manna House, you ask them to leave so that they won't endanger people. Truthfully that doesn't happen as often as you might think. There's a culture on the street, and they appreciate Manna House for what it is, and they give off the message to people, don't mess this up for us. But if it does happen, you can ask volunteers to help you, and you can call 911 if that's what you need to do to solve the problem."

She paused, then said, "So, are you in?  Are you ready to commit to a night at Manna House that you'll call your own?"

There was a silence in the room for a minute. All the nervousness that Clare had been feeling before she got to the training came rushing back. As Clare hesitated, she thought - 'I'm scared - but I came this far, I need to try.'  It felt like one of those things she'd regret not doing more than she was afraid of saying yes.

"Yes," Clare said, in a voice that was quiet but as sure as she could make it.

"Yes," Lisa said.

"Any preference for Thursday or Friday?"  Clare hesitated. She didn't have any social life to speak of at the moment, but did she really want to give away Fridays forever?

Lisa spoke first, looking at Clare as if she'd spoken her thoughts out loud. "You're young, and I remember what it was like to be young. Let me take Fridays, and you take Thursdays. Sound okay to you?"

"Thanks, that sounds great."

"Great, let's go over and take a quick tour before you go. Oh, and I'll need you to sign for us to do background checks. As soon as we get them in, you'll be on your own."

They walked out of the huge church building over the brick cross walk toward a yellow house Clare hadn't even noticed when she pulled up. It had an inviting looking front porch, with a large overhang that she could imagine filled with people avoiding the heat of the sun before dinner. There was a small sign carved out of wood hanging on the door that said, "Welcome to Manna House." Clare was impressed by how warm and friendly this place looked. Not institutional at all.

The three of them went in and saw that the house had been remodeled to be one large room, attached to one large kitchen. Off to the side there was what appeared to be a small den. Clare moved instinctively toward it, and Pam said, "That was a weight bearing wall, so we couldn't tear it down. Turned out to be a good thing actually. We needed someplace to keep the board's paperwork, all the grants we've applied for. Those, and some books people donate live in there. Some of our guests do borrow the books from time to time."

Clare looked at the books and noticed Dr. Seuss. "Children's books?"

"I guess I should have mentioned that we do of course have children here too. Families become homeless, and they need a place to eat as well."

Homeless kids – what would that be like? "Do they go to school?"

"Yes, there is a law that says you can go to the school you were at before you became homeless. The state is supposed to make that happen with transportation. It's still illegal to keep school age kids home from school, even when you don't have a home."

Looking around the empty room Clare imagined the people she was going to meet. She realized saying yes to this might turn out to be really painful. But she wasn't about to change her mind now. Whatever this Manna House thing turned out to be – Clare didn't want to be a person who wouldn't even try to handle it.

# Chapter 5

As usual, Clare slept in on Sunday morning. Then, she went to the Laundromat, and had way too much time to think. 'What if the people at Manna House don't relate to me? Or what if the volunteers resent me telling them what to do, because I'm too young? And what if that thing she said hardly ever happened happens, and I have to figure out what to do with someone who's high.' Clare went back home with clean laundry, but in a pretty agitated state. It was about 4:30, when she was literally pacing the floor of her apartment, that it hit her that the church sign had mentioned a service at 5:00. Without giving herself time to think about it, she got up and went.

The parking lot had some cars in it, which made her happy, because her goal was to be right on time – not early, and definitely not late. The sanctuary was kind of dark. It looked as though they had the lights on but turned down on a dimmer. There were candles lit in one section, so Clare went toward the light. A girl who looked to be about sixteen handed her a program and she went to sit in what she hoped wouldn't be somebody else's seat – in the middle row.

There was a pianist playing something she didn't recognize. The music was intricate and soft at the same time. Closing her eyes, she could hear every note. After awhile, her breathing slowed down, in rhythm with the music.

After a few minutes the voice of what must be the minister said, "Welcome to this service of worship. We are gathered here tonight to share in a time of quiet, a time of meditation, and a time of prayer. If you are new here tonight, we want you to know how glad we are that you are here. The program you have in your hand will guide you. One more explanation - the songs we sing tonight are really meant to serve as prayers. They repeat one verse over and over, so that eventually you are singing them from your heart as a prayer, rather than from your head. We just want to invite you to participate as you feel ready."

There were some people behind Clare, and some in front of her. The room didn't feel very full, which she liked. And she didn't feel like being alone made her stick out either. Maybe eventually she'd want to meet other people, but tonight she just wanted to slow herself down and breathe in the quiet of this room.

The people started singing a song Clare didn't recognize. It was pretty easy, and she felt comfortable joining in about the third time they sang it. Then everything got very quiet, and the minister read from a Psalm, about souls thirsting after God. Staring at the candle's flame, watching it burn, everything was silent. Then the pianist played again, and it was like the music was filling her up. The music felt like more than music. It was as if the young man was praying with the piano.

Almost against her will, Clare found herself comparing it to Danny's music. Danny had this same gift – to take music and make it part of your soul. But then she willed herself to put that thought aside and brought herself back to the room she was in.

More music, more Psalms, more quiet. Never had Clare been to a church service like this – where God seemed present in the quiet.

Then the minister went over to the candles and began to put them out. 'No' Clare wanted to say. 'Don't do that – I love the candles. I want to picture them burning there forever.' And he looked at them, and he said, "You are the light of the world," and she felt herself gasp – maybe not out loud, but she couldn't really be sure. Suddenly, the words connected with her in a way they never had before. The candles aren't out – that's what he was saying. The candles aren't out as long as she was part of the light of the world. The flames in here could be part of her life out there. She could choose to be somebodies' light.

No longer worrying about anonymity, Clare got up slowly, and filled out a card she found in the back of the sanctuary, giving them her name and e-mail. She knew she would be back.

# Chapter 6

When she got the quick yes on the Manna House background check – Clare felt the adrenalin kick in. Thursday finally came, and Clare left work a little early, to have as much time as possible to figure out what she was supposed to do. The area was quiet when she drove up. Hard to believe there'd be about a hundred hungry people arriving in an hour.

Almost as soon as she walked in, Clare heard a knock at the back door. "Hello – anybody here?"

She opened the door, saying, "Hi, I'm Clare. I'm the new Thursday night host."

"Hi Clare. I'm Sarah. Good to meet you," said the first woman with the aluminum foil food containers in hand. "We're First Baptist, and we've been coming here every quarter for a couple of years now. We've got Baked Ziti and warm bread. Are the ovens warm?"

Oops. "They will be." Clare ran to turn them on.

Turning back to the woman Clare said, "Baked Ziti and warm bread, that sounds great."

"Well, we'll see if you think it tastes great after you try some." She was laughing as she said it – a big warm friendly laugh. The woman put her food in the oven and motioned for everyone else to do the same. Then, without any directions, they started setting the tables. Clare felt lucky to have such an experienced group for her first night.

"So, you're new around here?"

"Yes, I just finished training this Saturday."

"Wow, that is new. We're used to having different people every time we come – Board members I guess? I heard they were trying to get more permanent volunteers."

"That's what they told me as well."

"Well, the only advice I have for you is get out of the way when you unlock the door." She laughed again, and Clare smiled. She could hear that there were people at the front door now – and checking the clock - she could see that it was just about time to open up. With a deep breath - Clare opened the door and was immediately overwhelmed with what one hundred people trying to get a shady spot on the porch looked like. She opened the door wide, saying, "Welcome to Manna House." She'd kind of practiced that, hoping it sounded like she was welcoming guests.

The first person through the door had on two layers of clothes - even though it was 80 degrees. Two pairs of pants, two shirts, a scarf, and he was pulling a bag behind him. It was an old suitcase on wheels that had rips along the edges that were fixed with duct tape. He looked at her with slight curiosity. Clare tried to speak, to welcome him, but nothing came out. He kept going right past her to the food.

Clare felt embarrassed, because she knew why she'd suddenly become mute. This was a man whose eyes she would never have had the courage to meet on the street. In here, in the light, it didn't seem like she should be afraid, but clearly, she was. Clare felt disappointed in herself.

Vowing to do better - she turned back to the line.

Next came a woman with a shopping cart full of what most people would call junk. She struggled to get it through the door – while the people behind her loudly told her to get a move on.

Looking up, she yelled – "I'm getting it – just hold your horses. The food's not going any place." Clare tried again to speak.

"Yes – there's plenty of food," she said. Clare reached out to help her move her cart, and the woman let out a shriek.

"Get away. It's mine." She screamed.

Clare pulled her hand back as if she had been burned. The people behind the woman shook their heads at her. "You can't touch Jeannie's cart. Not ever. You must be new."

Clare stepped back nodding her head that she was new – panicking now about what might go wrong next.

That's when Sarah from the church intervened. She took Clare's hand and brought her to a woman further back in the line saying, "Clare meet Velma. Velma's the unofficial dinner host."

Velma smiled at the title and smiled at Sarah too.

"Hi! You're new right?"

Velma looked to be about fifty. She had on jeans and a T-Shirt with a beach scene.

"Yes, this is my first night," Clare replied.

"Well, it's a good place." She said. "I think you'll like it." She kept moving while she was talking, smiling at her the whole time.

Suddenly Clare felt something hit her about knee-level, and looked down to see two kids, who looked to be trying to give her a hug.

Bending down to see them she said, "Hi, I'm Clare. Who are you?"

"I'm Eduardo, and this is my sister Paola." These children were little, maybe kindergarten age. They had huge smiles on their faces, and immediately Clare wondered about their story, but not out loud.

From her place in the line, a young Latina woman motioned to the children to join her. Clare walked over with the kids and introduced herself.

"Hi, my name is Clare Wheeler. I've just been meeting Eduardo and Paola. Are these your beautiful children?"

The woman flushed at the compliment and pushed her hair away from her eyes. "Yes. I'm Maria, their Mom. They are pretty friendly," she acknowledged. Clare could tell she didn't know whether to be proud or embarrassed by their behavior.

Trying to reassure her, Clare said, "I'm so glad to be meeting people. This is my first night, and I was hoping to learn some names and faces, so that next time, I won't feel quite so nervous."

"You're going to be back?"

"Yes, every Thursday night."

"So that's what's going on. I've been noticing some of the same faces, but we didn't know what was happening."

"They are trying to find hosts for each night of the week, so that our guests will get to know some of the same people if they come back. Do most of these people come back?" Clare asked, gesturing at the crowd.

Maria looked around. "I think I know most of the people here. Of course, every night they're a few new people, and lots of times people come once, on their way to somewhere else, but most of us come here for dinner pretty regularly." While they were talking Maria and her kids kept moving forward in the line, until they reached the buffet table with the food. Just then, the door opened and one more person, who must have been running late, came through.

"Mom, mom, it's Gus." The children left their places in line and ran to give a hug to the older man who'd just entered. Maria smiled, then called them back to get food with her.

Clare walked to the back of the line and introduced herself to the latecomer. "Hi – welcome."

"Thank you." The man the kids had called Gus smiled at her.

"I'm Clare Wheeler. I'm the new Thursday night host."

"I'm Gus. Nice to meet you. Great. They found somebody for Thursday nights. Do you know if they have a Friday person yet?"

"As a matter of fact, I do. Her name is Lisa, and she's starting tomorrow." Clare wondered how he'd known they were looking for somebody.

He nodded, then said, "I think it's a good idea, whoever came up with it. Makes it feel more homey, particularly for the kids, you know?"

Just then, a couple more kids came over.

"Did you know he's named after a month on the calendar?" one said.

Gus laughed at her confused expression. "August's my real name. Jeremiah thinks that's cool." There was something different about this man - in a room full of people, she could already tell that he was some kind of leader. Or at least people looked at him that way, and he seemed to accept the responsibility. If she had to guess, Clare would say he was about fifty, though that could be the aging of his face from spending the day outside. His hair was the definition of salt and pepper, and his eyes had the look of someone who was always paying attention to whatever was happening right in front of him.

Clare smiled, feeling a little more at ease. There weren't too many kids, but enough to see that this group seemed to really like the children. People all over the room were calling out greetings to the kids, and even offering to share their bread and butter with the ones who didn't like the Baked Ziti.

As the dinner progressed, Clare wandered through the tables, learning names, and seeing what was missing on the table that she could get. Velma asked for hot sauce, and Clare found some in the backroom. As soon as she had it, other people asked to borrow it too. The church group had interspersed themselves at different tables and were talking with the more outgoing guests. It impressed Clare that they did that; they didn't just bring the food and try to hide – they sat down and ate and talked with people too.

The meal wound up in about an hour, and then some of the guests kind of hung around for another half hour helping to clean up and put chairs away and chatting with each other. The more Clare watched them, the more she understood that this place was more than where they came to get food.

Clare couldn't have said what she'd been expecting exactly, but this was much more than whatever she'd had in mind. It was like she'd just found out a whole new world existed – on a parallel plane from the one where she'd been spending her time.

She got out her phone as soon as she walked into her apartment - wanting to connect with Kate. But for some reason - when her sister picked up - she suddenly didn't want to talk about Manna House at all.

"Hey Kate. How are you?"

"Cold – you don't have to rub it in."

"Hey! I didn't even ask this time."

"Yeah – but I knew you were thinking it."

"How's law school going? Any good arguments you want to share?"

"Actually, Matt and Sherri broke-up yesterday because they didn't agree on capital punishment. It was one of those days when I was glad I grew up in a family like ours. We knew how to have different opinions without forgetting we loved each other."

"Well, to be fair, that is a pretty big thing to disagree about. I don't think I could date somebody who thought capital punishment was a good idea either."

"See Clare – its comments like that that explain why your dating life is a lot more depressing than it should be."

"Isn't the point of dating to find someone you want to spend your life with? Why would I waste my time with somebody who doesn't even agree with me on the big stuff? Arguing over what's the best television show – sure. Arguing over who makes the best pizza – that's fine. But the life or death values stuff – those are non-negotiables."

"You lost me at 'the point of dating is to find someone you want to spend your life with.' Personally, I think the point of dating is to get to know somebody, have fun together. Every dinner and movie date doesn't have to be leading to the rest of your life. Some of them are just dinner and a movie."

It amazed Clare sometimes that she and Kate came from the same family. They'd always been so different. But – that's what Clare loved about being with her. Kate seemed like she enjoyed life in ways Clare didn't know how to do. She wondered how she could learn how to be a little more one day at a time about things - the way Kate was.

Kate's voice interrupted her thoughts

"You know Clare – what I actually need from you is one of your big sister pep-talks."

"Why – what happened?"

"Nothing really. I just keep feeling like I'm drowning in books, and I can't remember why I'm putting myself through this. I mean really - why didn't I just get a job out of college - instead of going through this three-year marathon for my brain?"

"Kate – since the day you first saw a lawyer on television standing up for the underdog and actually winning - you knew that was who you wanted to be. It was like you were born to do it. Don't let anything or anybody - including yourself - get in your way now. You've got this. Now get off the phone and get back to work."

"Wow – that was pretty good."

"Yeah – especially on short notice. Give me a warning next time, I could give you a whole speech."

"Thanks Clare."

"Anytime. Anytime."

They hung up and looking at the clock – Clare smiled to realize that in their own way - she and Kate balanced each other out. A lot of the time - they were just what the other one needed.

# Chapter 7

On Monday morning at Shepherd's Center, Clare was about three quarters of the way through piecing together the records when she came across a check made out to August Andrews. It might not have come to her attention, except for the fact that it wasn't accounted for in any of the columns, so it was one of the reasons the books were out of balance. Anyway, it seemed odd because she'd never heard the name August before, now twice in a week. It felt like a weird coincidence. The check was for $1200 - not exactly the amount of money a homeless man would have access too. She flipped it over, and saw that it was endorsed on the back, just with a name, no other information.

Finishing up balancing the month – Clare took a short list of checks for Susan to look at, to see if she could decipher where she needed to put the expenses.

Susan shook her head as she looked down the list. "For this accounting system to have worked, you'd have to be in a place where you don't get interrupted. And that's not this place! Here, interruptions are important. Lots of times, it's the people that interrupt me in the course of the day that need help the most."

Clare thought about that for a minute. In Clare's line of work, interruptions tended to be unbillable time, and so by definition, no one thought of them as a good thing. And in school, Clare had always needed uninterrupted time to get things done. But what Susan said about interruptions being important - Clare had never thought about that before. Could it be that the interruptions she'd always found annoying had sometimes been more important than what she'd been doing?

Clare said, "It's okay Susan. We just need something from your files, or worst-case scenario, from your memory, that would tell us where these should go." She watched her look down the list, putting something by most of the lines, and getting receipts to backup her work. But at the $1200 she stopped.

"This one – I remember it. See how there's no address on it. Just a name."

"I thought that was strange."

"Anyway, one of the therapists asked me to write checks to this man every so often, instead of taking a paycheck. It is a pain in the neck, because I have to go back and enter it into the pay records – it still needs to go on his W-2. I don't know why he doesn't just cash his paycheck and give the person the money. Now I know what to do when he asks me to do that, but at first, I guess I just didn't do anything at all."

"That does seem strange. Which therapist was it? I'll need to put it against his payroll account, to make things balance."

"Dr. Porter. Dr. Tom Porter."

Clare went back to her room, more curious than she had been before. Who was this Tom Porter? Why would he do such an odd thing – having his paycheck issued to someone else? It sounded like a way to avoid taxes, but if it was, it hadn't worked, since Susan had recognized the need to put the money in his W-2.

By the time Thursday came, Clare was almost finished with the Shepherd's Counseling job. It had been a huge challenge; she felt good about having been able to make order from the chaos.

"Susan, I won't be back tomorrow. I think I've got what I need. Thanks so much for everything. You've been great to work with."

Susan smiled, "Thank you. I was expecting a lot of reprimands, which I fully deserved. Thanks for pretending that it wasn't as bad as we both know it was."

Clare was on her way out the door, when a distinguished looking man almost knocked her over. She looked back at him, holding back a smile at the strange sight of a man that well-dressed running like a teenager late for school. That's when she heard Susan greet him, "Dr. Porter relax – your two o'clock called to say she was running late too."

Dr. Porter – the man with the check that didn't make sense. Clare still had the feeling something odd was going on with that. But she was convinced it wasn't the Counseling Center that was behaving strangely. At least now she had a face to put with the name that had bothered her.

As soon as Clare got in her car, she began to make the switch from accountant to Manna House host. These people had been on her mind all week. She'd be copying documents – and replay the moment at the front door when she couldn't get any words to come out of her mouth. She'd be preparing a list of questions for Susan and wondering what people like Velma did all day.

On her way in she noticed a youngish man coming toward her.

"Hey lady?" He said.

"Yes?" Clare asked. Clare glanced around, wanting to feel safer than she did.

"I was just wondering if anyone can come in here?"

"Yes – we open at six and everybody's welcome."

"Great!" He acted genuinely excited. It felt odd. He didn't look like any of the people she'd met the last time.

He seemed to sense her question. "I'm just passing through. I'm sort of a free-lance mechanic. I come into town, fix cars till I have money enough to keep going. Can't stay in one place for long. It's just the way I am."

It was the first time anybody had shared some of their story with her. It wasn't much as stories go, not a lot of drama, but she got it. This guy couldn't stand still – even if it meant he was hungry, he was going to keep moving.

"I need to go in and get things ready. I'll see you later," she said. Clare went in locking the door behind her. The volunteers came, and since there was no one with Sarah's outgoing personality, Clare knew that she was going to have to do a better job with being hospitable. She was prepared to welcome the new man at the beginning of the line, but when she opened the door at six, he was gone. And he never showed up while Clare was there. He'd seemed so happy about coming to dinner – it made her sad to think he couldn't stop moving even long enough to get a hot meal.

That night some of the same people came in again, and this time, her voice didn't desert her. She didn't always know what to say, but at least something came out. She decided her best chance of getting past "Welcome to Manna House," was with the children. She approached a table with a couple of the kids she'd seen the week before and said, "How's the chili?"

They smiled and nodded. "Good, really good. Did you make it?"

"Oh no" Clare laughed. "I'm not nearly this good at making chili."

"That's okay," the girl nodded. "Maybe they'll teach you." Her mother looked embarrassed, but Clare just smiled.

A volunteer called out from the kitchen, "Clare – the dishwasher's broken."  Her tone sounded like it was a crisis, a feeling Clare totally shared when she saw the pile of dirty dishes. Then she remembered her training – and found the circuit box, flipped a switch and the machine started running. The volunteers started clapping and cheering. Clare felt like a mechanical genius. This role was stretching her into a problem solver in ways she never expected.

# Chapter 8

Coming back to the office, Clare was pleasantly surprised to find out her supervisor Pete was so happy with her work on Shepherd's Center that he put a note in her file. He told her he wanted it on record that she was willing to stick with a problem until it was solved.

The next client paled in comparison. It was what the firm laughingly called "a bag job." Someone had come in the office with a bag full of receipts, deposit slips and cancelled checks, and asked to make a financial statement out of it, so that he could get a loan from the bank. The business was a small shop on St. Armand's circle, that sold sunglasses and hats to tourists, and judging by their deposit slips, there were a lot more tourists who came unprepared for the sun than Clare would have ever guessed.

By Thursday, she was so tired of looking at little pieces of paper; she couldn't wait to get to Manna House. At the front of the line this week was a woman who said her name was Tanya. She dressed better than everybody else, but when the food got put on the table, she ate as if she hadn't eaten in a very long time. Clare gave her a card that had Manna House hours on it, so she'd know she'd never have to be this hungry again.

Since this group brought more experienced volunteers, Clare got a chance to sit and share the meal with Maria and her two adorable kids. As usual the kids were greeting everyone as if they were family. "They need people," she said, shaking her head. "They don't like it being just us. I wasn't always on my own. Roberto and I we met up in Wimauma, and we got married. We had the kids and we were surviving - we had to go for help for food, but we had a room - it was okay. We were okay. And then six months ago he just disappeared. I knew he had been upset about not making enough money to take care of us, but I never thought he'd just leave. We loved each other so much." There were tears right under the surface. When Clare thought about it - she realized that Maria always had the eyes of someone trying not to cry.

"Do you think maybe something happened to him?" Clare asked tentatively.

"Maybe. But I hope not. I hope he left me – because if he left me – he could still decide to come back." She closed her eyes a little, and Clare instinctively put her hand on her shoulder.

"I hope so too." Clare said. However bad off they'd been before, Roberto would have provided them with more security. Being a single mom on the streets was such a vulnerable thing to be.

As if he could read her thoughts, Gus appeared. Gus seemed to have eyes in the back of his head where all the kids were concerned.

"Maria," he said.

"Yes Gus?"

"Don't let the kids run around tonight." She looked up, and Clare did too, and they both saw the reason for Gus' concern. There was a stranger at the door, a big man, who was walking unsteadily. Clare motioned to one of the volunteers and they went together to the man.

"Are you okay sir?" Clare asked.

"I'm okay. I just need something to eat." His words were clear, but his walk was still unsteady. She helped him toward a table, and the other volunteer went to get him some food. The man didn't say much – but every so often he'd make a noise, that sounded like he was in pain. People kept attending to him, but he didn't tell anyone what was wrong, and as soon as he finished eating, he left.

Gus kept looking around, as if he thought something was off.

Suddenly, he went to the back, toward the kitchen. Clare was right behind him, when he turned to call out for her.

"Clare – look at that."

She looked in the kitchen and saw that he was pointing in the direction of the coat closet. The shelves where people put their purses was empty. Looking down, the purses were on the ground, clearly dumped out in a hurry. And the back door was swinging in the wind.

Gus said, "Whoever it was is gone. I think the big guy was a diversion – so we'd all be looking the other way."

Clare felt sick to her stomach. She gathered the group leaders and told them that someone had gotten into their things. Then she called the police, and as soon as they came, the guests asked if they could go. One of the policemen said, "Yes, if you don't think any of them could have done it." Clare assured him they couldn't have – the logistics didn't make sense. The policemen watched as the volunteers went through their belongings, and ended up with six wallets missing, including credits cards and a total of about $450.

Someone asked, "Was the closet locked?"

"No." Clare shook her head.

"Well, it should be," said the policeman.

"I guess so," she said. It made her sad – but she knew he was right, it wasn't a good idea to tempt people who were struggling. Who knows, maybe whoever did this had watched them not lock up before and came up with this plan.

The volunteers were furious, and Clare couldn't blame them. Trying to do the right thing and getting rewarded by being robbed – not to mention the pain in the neck of getting new I.D - this was not what they'd signed up for.

Prepared for the leader to bite her head off, she approached him, but he managed a smile, saying, "We'll be back next month. I'm not sure some of these people will come back, but the whole church isn't giving up on helping just because somebody did a rotten thing."

Clare was so relieved that she wouldn't have to cross this church off the volunteer list that it took her a minute to absorb what he had just said to her. That he knew there would be new volunteers from his church, even after this happened - that was amazing to her. Clearly these people knew what commitment was all about, on a level she'd never seen before.

Clare thought she'd finished handling this whole nightmare, when it occurred to her that she probably wasn't supposed to be the only one who knew this happened. On the wall was a board member on call list, and she called the top name. There was no one there, but she left her message, complete with the name of the police officer that'd taken the information. She closed the door behind her, suddenly very aware of the darkness. Clare's hand shook so much she could hardly get the key into the hole to lock the door. All the way through the crisis she'd been brave and calm. But now, alone in the dark, the knowledge that she'd been so close to someone who wouldn't hesitate to take what he wanted - she was suddenly so on edge that tears stung her eyes.

If she hadn't been so jumpy, Clare probably wouldn't have even seen Gus, standing behind the corner of the building. He was watching her, and when she got in and started her car, he picked up his bag and left. Apparently, Maria and the kids weren't the only ones Gus was looking out for.

# Chapter 9

Clare woke up at least five times during the night. The Manna House robbery had definitely gotten to her. When the alarm went off, she got out of bed with a groan, hoping that the day wouldn't bring any challenges her tired brain wasn't ready for.

Pete was standing at her desk when she got in. He had a huge file in his hand. "Hi Clare."

"Good morning Pete. What's that?"

"It's a new client file. You and I are going to go out on the road next week."

"Both of us?"

"Yup. This is a client the partners want to impress, so they want us to come in looking really professional. You should be honored. You're the one I picked for the job. After the good work you did on the counseling center file, this is sort of a reward. High visibility and all that."

"So, stop keeping me in suspense. Who's the client?"

"It's the Ringling Museum." Pete looked proud to reveal the name. Clare was surprised. This was definitely a client outside their normal client list. She would have expected them to use a nationally known firm.

"Oh, I love that place! It's on my list of places to take people when they come to visit. That's awesome that we got that account!"

"Well, as of now, we're just auditing one transaction that they had."

"What?"

"Yeah, they've had some work done, and they think the contractor cheated them, and they want us to audit that job. But if they like us, we could get the whole thing – word is this is a test."

"Okay, now I'm nervous."

"Well, that's what this file is about. It's a process for auditing contracting jobs, a bunch of information on what the going rate is for the kind of work they had done, everything you need to be prepared for Monday morning. You can take it home with you; there's too much to read in one day."

Clare said, "Thanks Pete, for the opportunity. I really appreciate you taking me with you."

Looking through the file, the specifics of the project contained numbers with way more zeroes attached than she was used to seeing. Along with the complaints of the museum about the billing they'd received, there was construction industry lingo to decipher. Clare realized her short-term goal was to read enough to avoid looking stupid to the Ringling Brothers people.

Ready for a break, she decided to give Kate a call, but she didn't pick up. Then she tried her parents and had to leave a message too. Hm. Was everybody else busy on a Friday night? She finally decided to try calling old friends from college. For a long time, she'd been uncomfortable doing that because people always asked about Danny. But at this point most people already knew. A couple people picked up, and a couple of others got right back to her. Turns out there were other people who moved far away after school and were also sitting home on a Friday night, which made Clare feel more normal. Everybody she reached sounded happy to hear from her - and by the end of the last phone call, when one old friend after another asked to visit her in the wintertime - she remembered a little bit of the feeling she had when she chose Florida in the first place. Palm trees and sunshine and sandy beaches - sometime soon she needed to visit that Florida that was only a few miles from her front door.

Monday morning, Clare got to work early, and she and Pete went together to the museum. The offices were gorgeous, with big windows that gave views in every direction. They dug into the work together, preparing questions for both parties to this transaction, as well as completing a thorough reading of the clauses that provided for extra costs on the job. By the time they'd spent several days there, they both knew what the truth was – but neither one of them wanted to say it.

Finally, on Friday afternoon, Pete looked at her. "The bottom line is, the contractor was right."

"Yes." Clare knew this wasn't the answer anyone had been expecting.

"These exception clauses were met – every one of them. Ringling Brothers needs to pay the overruns."

"That's what I think too."

Looking down, Pete shook his head back and forth.

"Any chance you think they'll hire us as their firm, when we tell them we're on the other guy's side?" Clare tried to lighten the mood.

"I'd say no chance of that whatsoever. Plus, I'm sorry to say, I don't think the firm's going to appreciate our findings either." Pete actually looked a little pale.

"Well, what are we supposed to do? We can't falsify this." Clare could hear her accounting professor in her ear, saying, 'once you lose your integrity, you've got nothing left to offer in this profession.'

"I'll write up the report and give it to the partner. Whatever they say to us, I think we've done good work here, and ultimately – that's what should matter. The museum ought to be happy to know they didn't get overcharged. That's the way I'm writing it up."

"Okay. Do you want my help?"

Pete shook his head. "No, go ahead and take the rest of the weekend off. I've got it from here."

# Chapter 10

Clare realized that her schedule had been getting busier when she suddenly remembered on Sunday evening that she'd gone several days without returning one of Kate's calls. She picked up the phone and got ready for a little bit of nagging. But instead Kate sounded concerned.

"Hey Clare, I'm glad you called. Are you okay?"

"I'm fine. I've been pretty busy with some interesting stuff at work, and then Manna House on Thursdays."

"Oh, that's right. I forgot. Okay that's good." Her words were okay, but her tone was off.

Clare asked, "Kate is something going on?"

There was a long silence, until finally Kate answered.

"I don't want to tell you something, but I think it's better if you hear it from me."

That sounded ominous. Clare said, "Kate just tell me. You're scaring me."

"Well I ran into Elizabeth downtown the other day." Elizabeth was Danny's sister. Clare had forgotten she went to school in Boston too.

"Oh. That's awkward."

"It started out awkward then it got worse. Clare, she told me Danny's getting married."

The pain was immediate. Like she'd been punched. She realized after a minute that Kate was still talking. She hadn't heard anything after married.

"So anyway, it's going to be soon. Are you okay? Was I right to tell you?"

"Of course, you were right to tell me. I would have been upset if I found out you knew and didn't tell me."

"But are you okay?"

"Honestly, not yet. It hurts a lot. But maybe this is good. Whatever little part of me that thought he might come back has to give up now." Until that moment she'd had no idea that that hope had still been living inside her subconscious somewhere.

"I'm sorry Clare."

"I know you are. Thank you. Really, don't worry I'm going to be fine."

Clare hung up. She believed what she'd said to Kate. She just wasn't there yet.

She looked around her apartment, suddenly very aware she was alone, and let the tears come.

# Chapter 11

On Monday, Clare went into the office, afraid to hear what happened when Pete gave the results to the partners. Pete didn't leave her wondering long. He buzzed her to come in his office right away.

"You're not going to believe this. They were actually happy with our work."

"The Partners?"

"Oh – no the partners were ticked off at us. Jack Anderson even wanted me to re-write the report so that it didn't sound so clear-cut. But there wasn't time, so we presented the one I'd done to the museum people. And you know what they said?"

"Well – you said they were happy, although that makes no sense."

"They said, 'Well good. We're glad to know we weren't cheated. Now we can pay them without any fears that we're mis-using donated money."

"Wow. That's great!"

"Not only that – they said we showed integrity by not just trying to tell them what we thought they wanted to hear, so they'd like to work with us more in the future."

"That's terrific. I'm really happy for you Pete."

"Be happy for yourself too. Robert, the partner who gave me this assignment in the first place, actually issued a memo to all the partners praising our work, using us as a model for how doing the right thing pays off."

Leaving the office, Clare almost literally ran into Jack, the Senior Partner who'd almost rewritten their report.

"Are you Ms. Wheeler?" he asked.

"Yes – I am Clare Wheeler."

"Pete speaks highly of you."

"Thank you, sir. He's been a great person to learn from."

Jack nodded his head, started to move on, and then looked back.

"Ms. Wheeler, the work you did was good, but I wonder if you realize that accounting is an art – not a science. I hope you begin to get a better sense of how to make the numbers say what they should say. Otherwise, you're going to find it hard to get ahead around here." He turned and walked away.

Clare felt her cheeks turning red. They might have looked good in some people's eyes, but clearly Jack Anderson was less than pleased.

# Chapter 12

The office was getting busier and busier. Clare thought about whether she should be asking to be replaced at Manna House on Thursday nights for the couple of months of full on busy season that were coming up soon. She'd realized through coffeepot conversations that most of the other junior accountants in her firm planned to stop taking the night off they were allowed - to look good when the next senior slot opened. But Clare didn't want to go back to having life be all about work. So, she got up the nerve to tell Pete that she intended to keep taking Thursday evenings off. Apparently, Pete still felt like she was doing good work, because he didn't ask any questions, he just said, "If that's what you need – you've got it."

Clare felt so relieved that Pete hadn't gotten angry. She knew that the decision she was making was the right one for her, and it was within the rules - but still. She didn't want Pete to lose faith in her. And she wasn't used to going against the grain of what everybody else was doing. But inside, she knew that giving up her night at Manna House wasn't an option she wanted to take; she was glad she'd done what felt like the right thing to do. She went home from work at the end of the long day feeling almost content, looking forward to having the left-over pepperoni pizza she'd saved for dinner, and expected that she'd be tired enough to fall asleep sooner rather than later that evening.

The phone rang, and Clare picked it up without even glancing at who it was.

And then the world turned upside down.

"Clare?" She heard his voice - and she could hardly breathe. It had been so long - she didn't believe it at first.

"Danny?"

"Yes! Oh Man - it is so good to hear your voice. You sound - so good. So different."

"Really? You don't. Why are you calling me Danny?" She didn't want to talk to him. She really didn't. Clare felt as if her heart was getting squeezed in a vice.

"Well - I missed you. And I heard you were down in Florida - and I'm on my way there and..."

"Kate told me you're getting married. So, if that's what you felt like you wanted to tell me - I already know."

"Yeah - I'm supposed to be getting married. In the summer."

Almost against her will, Clare asked "Supposed to be? What does that mean?"

"Well - you know - I mean it's happening. There's a park, and bridesmaids, and a picnic and the whole bit."

"Great!  Good luck with all that."  She wanted to hang up - but she didn't.

"So anyway - I just - I'm playing in Sarasota in a couple of days, and I wanted to see you. I hate the way we ended things Clare. I mean that was three years of both of our lives. It shouldn't just end like it wasn't important."

Now Clare felt angry - exactly who did he think made it seem unimportant?  She didn't speak - she let him keep going.

"Do you think we could maybe get a drink after the set my band is playing on Friday?  We're opening for somebody. We could meet at one of those places by the beach. Kind of put our whole thing in a better place. What do you think?"

'Say No!' said every bone in Clare's body. But what she said to Danny was "Sure. I'll text you a good place. What time will you be done?"

"Eleven. Thanks Clare. That's awesome. I'll see you soon." He hung up - in a hurry. Probably afraid she'd change her mind. Which she should - but she wouldn't. She knew that already. Once she'd said yes - she knew she wanted to see him. Maybe just to have a better good-bye, maybe to ask him all those questions she never got a chance to ask.

# Chapter 13

Clare left her office right at five on Thursday. She had a twinge of guilt, but by the time she got to Manna House, she felt at peace again. That is, until she got to Manna House and saw Gus waiting on the porch. She knew right away that something had to be wrong. Gus rolled up his pant leg to show her a wound that had definitely come from a knife, although he didn't give her any details.

"Come on in, Gus," She said. Gus didn't have a mean bone in his body, but apparently that hadn't stopped other people from fighting with him. Chances are - he'd been protecting somebody else. The wound didn't look infected – that was the good news.

Clare opened up the door for him to come in out of the heat. Not exactly within the rules, but she figured no one else would be there to catch her for half an hour – and by then, the doors would be ready to open anyway.

"Gus, go ahead and sit down over in that little library, if you want. It's more comfortable. You can even put your ankle up while you're waiting."

"Thanks Clare – I'm gonna do that."

She went over to the kitchen, flipped on the lights and looked at the directions for the night's dinner. Heat the oven to 350 degrees – and put in the trays of lasagna one of that night's volunteers had dropped off earlier. Then cut up the bread and put it in big baskets.

She was settling into a rhythm with cutting the bread when a noise came from the other side of the kitchen. "You need some water Gus?" Clare called out.

"I could use some water – but I'm not Gus." She looked up to see a man who looked like he'd just come in from the beach. His hair was light brown, with blonde streaks that looked like they came from the sun and his skin was tan, the way people used to look before the advent of SPF 30. He had the long lanky build of a surfer – although if he was a surfer he was probably the serious kind. He looked too old to be a spring breaker.

"How did you get in here?" He didn't look particularly scary, but Clare suddenly felt pretty vulnerable.

"The door was open. I knocked but you probably didn't hear me."

"Oh." Clare thought she'd locked it back up, but clearly she hadn't. "Well, we don't open for another twenty minutes, but since you're in, why don't you just go wait in the lobby?"

"Looks like you have a lot to do. Could I help?" Clare'd been working at Manna House just long enough to know that lots of the new people said this. Especially the ones that felt like they should be earning their food

"You could set the chairs around the tables. Eight to every table." She liked the idea of him helping – in another room. He smiled and went. Clare had the feeling he knew why she gave him that job.

Clare went back to cutting the bread, smelling its fresh scent with every stroke of the knife. Then it occurred to her that she hadn't been as friendly as she should have been to a guest. A new visitor to Manna House should have been received as a guest. She'd treated him with suspicion - not remembering how tough it was for people to go through those doors for the first time - to ask for help. She hated that her fear had gotten in the way of being hospitable.

Trying to think of a way to start over – she remembered that when she thought he was Gus and asked him if he wanted water, he said yes. Glancing at the clock, Clare saw she was ahead of schedule, and went to get a glass to take to the mystery surfer man.

He already had the chairs almost set-up. Just as she came in the room with the water, there was a knock on the outer door. He looked up and saw her, so she motioned that the water was for him, and went to get the door, wondering who else was early for the evening meal.

The people at the door definitely weren't guests. Their well-pressed clothes, leather shoes and designer bags made that obvious. There were three of them, two women and a man.

"Can I help you?" Clare asked.

One of the women spoke up. "We're here for a meeting." A meeting – during dinner hour at Manna House? That didn't sound like a very good plan – the noise and the traffic in and out of the small building would make conversation pretty tough. But these people seemed to be confident that they were in the right place, so she opened the door wide to let them pass.

"Where were you supposed to meet?" Clare asked. Her skepticism probably showed on her face, because the second woman smiled at her, and answered both her spoken and unspoken questions.

"Right here dear. We're members of the Manna House Board, and we're here to meet someone, but we also just wanted to see the mission in action."

Clare held out her hand to the first woman saying, "I'm Clare Wheeler. I'm the Thursday night host."

They introduced themselves to her in turn - Pauline Gephardt, Timothy Connor, and Melinda Wainwright. Clare decided to use Ms. And Mr. and concentrate on remembering the last names. They didn't feel like people she'd be getting to know on a first-name basis.

"Well – I'm almost ready to open the doors, so why don't you go ahead and look around?" Remembering that two of the guests were already on this side of the door, Clare said, "I let a couple of people in early tonight. One's recovering from an injury, and the other's brand new, so I didn't want to ask him to leave – wouldn't be a very hospitable first impression." Recognizing that they were the body that made the rules, she hastily added, "Hope that's okay."

"Oh, we always rely on the judgment of the volunteer hosts. You know best what works here." Clare nodded in response to the man's comment, but he wasn't done. "Of course, having different rules different days could be confusing."

"Yes," She acknowledged. Her overly developed defensiveness gene tried to take over her brain and come back with some kind of rationalization that made her sound good. But she controlled that impulse, at least in part because he wasn't wrong, and she knew it.

They started into the other room, where "the surfer" was finishing getting the chairs set just right around each table. Clare was impressed with the care he was taking, spacing the chairs at even distances, avoiding the legs of the tables.

"Oh, my," said, Ms. Gephardt. "We put you to work already?"

"Wouldn't have it any other way," said the stranger.

Now Clare was really wishing she'd asked him his name. She couldn't introduce him to these folks as "the new guy," and certainly not "the surfer."

He bailed her out, going directly toward the board members with his hand out to shake their hands. He was sure more confident than the average guest.

"I'm Paul." He said. "Paul McLain."

"So good to meet you," said Ms. Wainwright. Her tone of voice told Clair something she hadn't considered before. She looked quickly around to see Paul McLain's face. He smiled slightly at her look, and she felt her face begin to grow hot.

Mr. Connor turned toward her. "Do you think we could meet in the library?" So, this was the person they'd come to meet with. Great! The guy was probably a donor, and she had treated him like someone who was there to hurt her.

"Sure. Gus is in there, but it's time for dinner, and so I'll just ask him to come out and get ready to get in line when I open the doors.'

Gus was already getting up when they came in. There was a clock on the wall, so he knew it was almost time to eat. The four of them closed the door behind them, but not before Paul McLain shook her hand, saying – "Thanks for the water, and the welcome." He actually seemed sincere.

No more time to think about what was happening in the library. Clare's schedule hadn't allowed for all these interruptions. The group that was supposed to help serve didn't come in until 5:55, but at 6:00 Clare opened the door to a line of people that looked a little larger than average. Gus knew better than to be waiting at the front of the food line. That would have caused some tempers to flare. Nothing like the sense that someone was getting preferential treatment to bring back the sibling rivalry memories that seem to lurk underneath the surface for everybody. Clare still remembered the "it's not fair" arguments she and Kate had. Watching the way things worked around Manna House, Clare wondered if maybe that "it's not fair," feeling was still there for most people - just buried under the pretended civility that life in the "functional" world demanded.

"Hi Clare."

"Hi Maria. Hi Eduardo – Hi Paola." How are you doing today?" Maria's little ones flashed their beautiful smiles in her direction. Clare thought again about how young they were. They didn't seem to realize yet that their lives were different from anyone else's, which must have been a real blessing for their Mom.

Behind Maria was a man who said his name was Tom. He had no problem sharing his story. In fact, he seemed to want to make sure that Clare knew that he hadn't always been on the street. He said he'd been walking on the sidewalk in downtown Sarasota, and a drunk driver hit him. "That guy took everything from me. My job, my money, my insurance ran out, my family. He's in jail - but at least he gets three meals a day. I'm out here, having to come to places like this." His words were angry, but Clare also saw that his eyes had tears in them. She listened, recognizing there wasn't really anything she could say to the pain he was talking about. She hoped that somehow the listening would help.

Tonight's lasagna was getting high marks from the guests. Clair could hear the buzz moving from the front of the line to the back. The volunteers were serving well, so she started circulating, talking to folks, and that's when she heard the rest of the buzz. "Hey Clare, what's with the fancy people in the library?" For the regulars, this was like someone coming into their home that they didn't know.

"They are board members," she said.

"Never saw them come around before." Clare wasn't surprised that Harvey sounded particularly negative about this. Whatever was going on in his life, part of the issue seemed to be some kind of paranoia – always looking behind him, never putting down his bag, even when he was getting his food.

"Really? I thought they used to run Thursday nights?"

"Not these people," said Velma, sharing a little of Harvey's worry.

"Well, okay – but I think it's a good thing they're here now. They want to see how things are working around here."

Clare watched the faces of the people around the table as they took this information in. Some of these men probably served on this kind of board in some long ago past – before alcohol took them over the edge. Others didn't remember what it was like not to live on the streets. Some of them probably never even considered what it took to get the food on these tables every night.

Clare gravitated over to Gus, to make sure he was eating. Sometimes, he was so focused on the kids that he didn't take time to eat himself. Clare wondered again what his story was. So far, Gus hadn't said anything about his life before she met him. She never smelled alcohol on him, although that didn't mean he wasn't a drinker. With Gus, Clare wanted to break the rules and ask questions. On the other hand, she really didn't want to scare him away, so she never even hinted that she wanted to know where he came from, and how he ended up on the streets.

"Gus – how's the lasagna?  Cooked the way you like it?"

"Sure Clare – it's just right. Bread's good too."

She noticed that the room had suddenly gotten quieter and turned around to see the board members and their mystery friend coming out of the library. They looked around and found a table with open seats, then went over to get a little food from the food line. They picked a table together, but they didn't pick one that was empty, which impressed her. Apparently, they did want to enter into the meal on more than an observer level.

She moved over to introduce them to the leader from the group who was helping out for the evening. "Sal, these are members of our Manna House board and this is… Paul McClain." She realized she still didn't have a clue about who Paul McClain was.

"Nice to meet you," said the male board member – whose name she was having trouble remembering. "I'm Tim Connor. Thanks for the work you're doing."

"Oh – our group loves to come," said Sal. "And Thursdays might be our new favorite night to help out – Clare has everything so under control."

Clare nodded her thanks, but felt embarrassed by his comment, especially since these same folks had caught her breaking rules when they came in. If her night was under control, what did the rest of the week look like?  Or at least that was what she was afraid they were thinking.

Clare suddenly recognized a bad feeling in the pit of her stomach. It felt like the "Mother Bear" feeling people talked about coming into their lives after they had kids. Like if anybody hurt their kids, all bets were off. Why was she feeling that right now?

# Chapter 14

Clare flipped the light switch to go into her apartment, sad that the times when the sun shone until well into the evening were past. At other times of the year, she could go for a walk in the evening, and let the ocean remind her how big life really is. Today seemed like a day that needed a big picture perspective.

She kept replaying everything she said all night, second-guessing every word. Why was she being so obsessive? The discomfort with the unexpected guests at Manna House didn't have to mean something sinister. Had she become such a control freak she couldn't handle a little surprise in her life?

Clare felt as though she needed something to counteract this feeling that would be called foreboding in the novels that used to be part of her daily life. Fiction – that was a lost love. Since she spent so much of her time reading little numbers at work, her eyes were too tired by the end of the day to read anything else. When she first started the job, she still tried to read – would be still doing it, except for her total lack of self-control. Once she entered a good book's world, she'd read through the night and then be useless in the morning.

Suddenly, Clare felt like she'd made a compromise for work that wasn't worth it. Without letting herself think twice about it, she got into her car, and went to The Little Shop of Books. It was one of the things she loved about this neighborhood when she found her apartment. Hardly any towns seemed to have small bookstores anymore. But in reality, she'd never even made time to go in.

Walking through the shelves of the small store felt a little like coming home again. She remembered losing herself for hours in a store like this in her hometown. The Bookworm, it was called. The owner never said a word when she rifled through book after book and stood and read chapters at a time. In the end, she always bought something – usually something too long to read standing up.

This bookstore had an organizational system that made Clare smile. Apparently, the diet and exercise self-help books were better sellers – they were all in the front of the store. After all, in Florida nothing could be hidden under bulky clothes, like back home. It took her awhile to find the fiction. The store had little tags under some of the books, with reviews that seemed to come from the owners, or maybe the workers. She got caught up in the reviews of an oddly titled book "The Guernsey Potato Pie Society."

"It's a good one – once you get into the style of writing."

Clare looked up, expecting to see someone who looked official – and found herself face-to-face with Paul McLain. Unbelievable. She was actually at the store to distract herself from the weird feelings she got at Manna House – and one of the sources of the weird feelings was standing right in front of her.

"It's a good book," he said again. "History, romance, intrigue, the whole package. Or at least that's what I thought. Not that my opinion is the same as other people."

"Well – apparently you agree with Diana and Sheryl – whoever they are." Clare pointed toward the review posted under the book. She suddenly had the urge to apologize to him. "Tonight, at Manna House. I could have been friendlier when I first saw you. I'm sorry."

"Oh – I understood. You were busy, without much time to get everything done, and I was an intruder. I scared you."

She didn't like that he knew she'd been scared – but he wasn't wrong, so she couldn't disagree without feeling like a fraud. She decided to change the subject.

"Did the meeting go well, with those Board people?"

"Actually, it did. But I was curious about something. It seemed like they didn't know you, but most of the guests knew you. Do those people not usually come to dinner?"

"Well, there used to be board members who came to dinner, but since I've been working at Manna House, I've never seen them on-site before. Maybe they feel like their role is to raise the money, and its other people's job to do the hands-on-work." She was surprised to find herself defending the board. "The other thing is – my night to be there is Thursday night, so I can't say for sure what happens other nights of the week."

"Still – I didn't notice any of the guests recognizing them either."

"That's true. I don't know what to tell you." If he was a donor, she had the feeling the answers she was giving him weren't passing his test. "Does that bother you?"

"It just means I might have more work to do than I imagined."

Clare had no idea what he was talking about, though he seemed to think she did. Deciding that bluffing would just leave her even more worried about what was going on, she said, "I'm sorry – I don't understand."

It was his turn to look flustered. "Oh. I guess I just assumed – but why would you know." He paused, and she could see he was deciding whether to trust her about something.

"You don't have to explain if you don't want to." 'Please want to' she silently willed him.

"No – I think it's okay. After all the confidentiality of these kind of things is usually set up to protect the person in my position. I'm interviewing to be the Director of Manna House."

"The Director? I don't think we've ever had a Director before."

"I know. That's why I was surprised you hadn't ever met the Board people before. Who's been doing the job they are hiring me for?"

"I don't know. What job are they hiring you for? I mean – what are they telling you, you'll be doing?"

"Coordinating provider groups, supervising volunteers, helping develop funding, and working with the guests to see if there's something we can provide for them – like connecting them with social services that might make their lives better."

Clare thought for a minute about what he was saying. Who was doing those things? On Thursday nights, she was doing some of them. She started to say that – then realized it might sound more defensive than she really wanted to be.

"Well – some of those things the evening directors like me help with. Some of them I guess the board has been doing. And some of them – no one is doing right now. Maybe a Director would be a good thing." She said this with as much enthusiasm as she could – but she wasn't feeling it. Clare liked Manna House the way it was. Clare loved Manna House the way it was.

She went on, "Not that I want to make you feel like you just walked into another interview, but would you mind telling me something about who you are? I'm a pretty curious person."

He smiled. "I think you're more than a curious person. I think you're a person who cares about Manna House, and you're hoping the Board isn't about to put someone into the mix who doesn't have a clue."

She couldn't keep herself from smiling back at him. "Well, clearly you're good at reading people's minds. That's a skill that must come in handy."

"I'm also pretty good at noticing what kind of people I might be working with – and you struck me as a person who cares about everything – the guests, the volunteers, the way things are running."

"Thanks. Manna House is a special place to me."

"It shows. Listen, I'm glad I ran into you – you've helped me answer some of the questions I had when I left the interview today. I've got to go now; I'm meeting some people for dinner."

He left, and she watched him go, feeling pretty good about the conversation. It was only after she bought the book, and went back home to curl up with it, that she realized Paul McLain hadn't told her one thing about himself.

# Chapter 15

The phone rang at the same time as her alarm, and in a confused daze Clare said out loud "Who calls somebody before 7:00 A.M., unless it's a real emergency?"

Then it hit her that it might be a real emergency, and she ran to catch the phone before it went to voicemail.

"Hello, can I speak to Clare Wheeler please?"

"This is Clare Wheeler."

"Are you the Clare Wheeler that runs the Thursday meal at Manna House?"

"Yes."

"I'm sorry to call you this early. This is Lisa from Manna House. I run the Friday night meal. Maybe you remember me from the training?"

"Of course."

"The thing is, I just got a call that I need to leave town because my mother's really ill. I wondered if you might be able to take my shift? Just for tonight."

So, it was an emergency – just not her emergency. Having been nervous for those few moments, empathy for Lisa came easy.

"Sure, I can do it. I hope your Mom is okay."

"Me too. We won't know for a while. If this is a longer-term thing, I'll call the Board and ask to be replaced, but I don't want to do that if I'm on the plane back here in a few days. Thanks – I really appreciate you doing this."

"No problem."  And it wasn't – because the plans Clare had for the night were the ones she'd been trying not to think about - meeting Danny at 11. Having something to do earlier was actually a lifesaver, in that she wouldn't be going crazy waiting all night for it to be late enough to go out. And it wasn't crunch time when people worked late on Fridays yet - so she wouldn't feel guilty leaving on time two days in a row.

"Don't worry, I've got it," Clare said, glad she could give Lisa space for whatever was happening with her Mom.

Clare put down the phone, and realized she needed to try to get to work early – just to make sure she wouldn't get dirty looks for leaving on time. Jumping in the shower, she felt a sense of happiness that seemed to be coming from the idea of an extra night shift at Manna House. Whatever today looked like at work, she knew the night ahead would bring a chance to see people who would be happy to see her, and that thought was one that would keep her moving through her day. Even knowing that Danny was on her agenda didn't take away her happiness, much.

Clare wasn't worried about taking over for Friday night, thinking that it would be the same as Thursday. But once she got to Manna House, the differences were obvious. For one thing, the guests seemed more nervous. Gus was there, looking like his ankle felt a little better, but he seemed jumpy too. She went over to his table and asked him about the feeling she was noticing in the air.

"Oh, everybody's nervous on Fridays. We have to figure out where to go for the weekend."

"What do you mean? Why is Friday night any different than the rest of the week?"

"Because on Friday nights, the tourists are all over the place, and nobody wants us to mess up the tourist business. So, the locals call the cops more, and the cops keep moving us out."

"But Gus, why don't people just go to one of the shelters?"

He looked surprised by the question. "Clare, there aren't nearly enough shelters for us if we all wanted to go, and most of us don't want to go anyway, because we feel like the shelters aren't safe. You get your stuff stolen, you can't sleep."

What he was saying didn't make sense to her. The shelters were more dangerous than the street? How could that be? Maybe it was just the perception – because on the street, you felt some kind of control – like where you slept was on your terms?

Then Clare noticed that over in the corner of the room was a young woman she'd never seen before. She looked maybe twenty-two or twenty-three. The raggedy edges of her hair made it look as though she'd cut it herself. As Clare looked at her, she realized the thing that bothered her most was the feeling she got when she looked in the girl's eyes. Like they were vacant - nobody inside. Could it be drugs, or maybe depression? Clare didn't know enough to know.

The girl didn't seem like she had any idea what to do. Clare spoke to her. "Would you like something to eat?"

The girl nodded but didn't move.

Clare motioned - "Over here. We have pasta with meat sauce tonight. Everybody says it good."

The girl moved, but there was a shakiness that made Clare nervous.

"So, I'm Clare Wheeler. Is this you first night at Manna House?"

The girl nodded slightly.

Gus - always with eyes in the back of his head - seemed to sense something was off about the conversation Clare was having. He came closer.

Just as he got close enough to hear - the girl's eyes got even wider. She turned to Clare and raised her hand as if she was going to slap her. Clare shrunk back.

"Leave me alone!" the girl screamed. The words seemed to come from deep in her gut. She ran to the door as if she was being chased and disappeared out it.

"What was that?" Clare said out loud. Then more quietly she said to Gus, "Drugs?"

"No way to know."

Clare said, "Have you ever seen her before?"

"Not exactly - but yeah." Gus' eyes were very sad.

"What do you mean by that?"

"Well," said Gus, "not her. No. But I've seen that look before. That girl's in a lot of pain." And suddenly Gus' eyes were filled with tears. In his hand, he held a plate of food. He looked at it, and then without another word he put it down. And he walked out the door.

Was he going to try to find her, Clare wondered? If so, she didn't think he'd have much luck, as the girl had been moving very fast.

The mystery that was Gus just kept getting deeper.

About half way through dinner, there was a bit of noise over by the front tables. Clare went over and found four men talking with a lot of animation, to someone she couldn't see at first. When she got closer, she saw it was Paul McClain. He looked up at her - surprised, and maybe a little uncomfortable - as if he'd been caught.

"I thought Thursday was your night," he said.

"It is. I've never been in on a Friday before, but the person who runs Fridays had an out-of-town emergency. What are you doing back here? Is there a phase two of your interview?"

"No. I just thought I'd stop by, before I go back home, and see what it was like here, without having to talk to board members at the same time." The men who'd been talking to him were backing away.

"Well don't let me interrupt you. It looked like y'all were having a good conversation." She tried to motion the others not to leave.

"Y'all? I would have thought you were a northerner."

"I am. But y'all is such an infectious phrase. It works in so many situations." She went back to talking with the guests - unexpectedly pleased that Paul McClain had come back to see the real Manna House. Maybe, just maybe the Board was going in the right direction after all.

And then as quick as the evening had started, it was over. Clare was left with her thoughts about the rest of the night. She had done a good job of distracting herself - but now it was time to face that the night in front of her would bring something she'd never really expected to have again - a moment in time with Danny.

# Chapter 16

Sitting and waiting - nothing new about that. Clare remembered sitting and waiting for Danny - always. She wondered if he'd ever sat and waited for her. His world wasn't based around clocks. That's what he used to tell her. At first that had sounded so artsy and appealing - so outside the lines of how she'd always seen life. Over time though, she had begun to wonder if it was only his relationship with her that existed in the time-free zone. He got to jobs on time, at least most of the time. He practiced with his band at the same time every day. He went to his classes. But when it came to her - he'd expect her to be wherever they were meeting, whenever he got there.

There was no doubt that Clare had put Danny on a pedestal. His gift for music had struck her as inspired, maybe even spiritual, though he would have never described it that way. When he was playing a light would go on in his eyes and she could tell that he had - well - left the room. No matter how many people were around, it was just him and his music. When he got to that point, and then he would stop playing, the clapping actually seemed to startle him.

Once she'd referred to his music as a gift from God. That had really not gone over well. He heard it as if she was saying he hadn't put in the work - which wasn't what she meant at all.

In the middle of her thoughts, Danny came through the entrance of the patio, looking for her. She saw him first, and she watched as he saw her, and his eyes lit up, with that smile that had always made everything okay in their world.

"So sorry I'm late Clare - the owner kept telling us how happy he was with our performance. I wanted to wait until the end of his praise, to see if he wanted to book us again."

"And did he?"

"He did. Not until next year though, and some of the guys are kind of nervous about booking that far out, so we ended up telling him we'd get back to him. But I'm sure it will happen. All I need is a couple of minutes to talk to them, and I think I can convince them that Florida in the winter is a job they want to say yes to." Danny pushed his hair back - he'd always kept his hair long. She used to tease him that he thought his talent was in his hair - so he was afraid to cut it.

"Congratulations."

"Thanks." He stopped then and looked at Clare with that look that had always convinced her she was the only woman in the world for him. Which at this moment - she found irritating, given that he was engaged to somebody else. She decided to go right toward that subject.

"So, Danny - who is the girl? She must be something if she got you to change from the musician who needed to be free of romantic entanglements in order to create?"

He looked off his game for a minute - confused by her words.

"Clare - I never said you got in the way of my ability to create."

"Okay, that's fair. You didn't say much of anything, except to tell me I wasn't "the one." I had to fill in the blanks in your explanation."

When he continued to look stunned - she kept going. "You look surprised. Did you think I was totally over how we ended? You've never tried to be friends with me before. Why did you want to see me now?"

Danny looked away, and then looked back. "I guess I was hoping for something that wasn't fair to hope for. That time would just make the whole lousy ending go away. But I'm here now - so go ahead. Ask me what you want to ask me. Yell at me, if that's what you need to do."

Suddenly - free to ask and to yell and to tell Danny the pain he caused her - she didn't want to say a word to him about any of it. She didn't want to share her feelings with him, even to try to make him feel guilty.

"I don't need to know anything now - I'm just as happy with the stories I told myself that helped me move on. Let's just leave that as the truth."

Danny's relief was visible. It was clear to Clare as she looked into his eyes that she would have found no peace in any story he would have told her. "So, can we try to have a friendly conversation?" He asked.

"Sure, what would you like to talk about?" The question had skepticism written all over it, but Danny chose to ignore that.

"Well - how's it going here for you?" Danny asked.

"I work a lot. I'm going to be working even more."

Clearly uncomfortable with her short answer, Danny kept trying. "Must be nice living here. What do you do for fun? Go to the beach?"

"I've been volunteering at a place that helps hungry people." Clare answered.

Danny couldn't have looked more surprised. Clare didn't even try to explain.

After a pause, she said, "You know - I'm serious - I would like to hear about this new woman in your life."

"Really?" He looked doubtful.

"Don't worry. I'll stop you if I don't want to hear any more."

"Okay - well Michelle is an artist. She paints - amazing stuff. In the style of the impressionists, but with contemporary topics - she's going to have a show up in Detroit - in the renovated section of the city, where they are opening galleries and coffee shops."

Surprisingly - nothing Danny was saying about Michelle bothered Clare at all. Michelle wasn't Clare - at a different time, in a different place. She was an artist - maybe a creative equal to Danny. Who knows - maybe even more talented in her field than Danny. That wasn't Clare. If he wanted a creative partner - he had been right that she wasn't "the one."

Still - something felt wrong about this whole conversation. And something felt wrong about Danny calling and asking her to meet him.

"She sounds great Danny. Really."

"She is. She's fantastic. I'm just not sure…"

"You're just not sure…about what?"

"Well - how we can actually make it work. You know? I mean who's going to be the one who makes the practical decisions? Who decides that we have to pay bills and you know - get a job that has a steady paycheck? And health insurance?"

Clare almost spit her drink out. "Did you just say health insurance? Who are you?"

"Yeah I know. But Michelle - she disappears into her studio for hours at a time - sometimes for days at a time. She's not going to think of any of this stuff."

"Okay - but you are engaged right?"

"Yeah."

"So - did this all just occur to you?"

"Well - kind of."

The light bulb was beginning to turn on. "So, you came to see me to help you figure out the practical part of your marriage to somebody else."

"Well when you say it that way it sounds terrible."

"But it is that way, isn't it?"

"No. No... It's just that I always really respected your brain. And when I was coming here - I just thought maybe I could talk to the smartest person I know - and maybe..."

"Maybe I'd solve your problems for you." The anger that had been under the surface the whole night began to rise in her chest, until she had to let it out. "You know what Danny - I will give you one clue. Talk to Michelle. Talk to her about the practical side of life. Make a plan with <u>her</u>. If you love her - give her a chance to be part of solving your problems together. And if you don't love her - well you are really good at leaving without feeling the need to explain. Just do what you did to me."

She grabbed her purse and left. By the time she got to the car, she could barely hold back the sobs that were trying to come out. She drove just as far as the next parking lot and let herself cry. The person who solves his problems - that's how he'd always seen her. Not as the woman he loved, but as the woman who was the adult, who could fix things so that he could keep being the child.

As the sobs slowed and she began to breathe, the words 'Never again' ran through her mind. Never again would she let this happen to her. If there was ever going to be another man in her life, he would be her partner, her equal. He would make her life better, he would push her to grow and be who she wanted to be. Everything she could be. And she would do the same for him. They would be a team. Otherwise - there was no point in having a relationship at all.

# Chapter 17

There was something in Clare that didn't want to share that night with anyone - even her family didn't need to know what she'd learned about who Danny really had been to her. She wasn't sure if she was embarrassed - or just didn't want to hear the anger and pain in everybody else's voice. On Saturday, she tried reading, but found herself too distracted to get into anything. Finally, she used the feelings she had to clean her apartment - scrubbing with all her strength.

Clare spent Sunday walking around Ringling Museum. She let the exhibits bring her into their world - which was good, because she really wasn't very happy in her own at the moment. She found herself driving to the church service on Sunday night - without even really making the conscious decision to go. This time she noticed that they had moved a big glass bowl of water up front. She looked around for a baby, since the only time she'd ever seen water in church there'd been a baby involved - but she didn't see anybody with kids in the room.

Then the Pastor got up - and said, "Today is the day we celebrate the new life that Jesus gives us in the waters of baptism. Every day is a new day, and we all get a chance to begin again. And who among us doesn't need that!" There was a murmur of agreement throughout the room.

"So, if you want to, anytime tonight - come up, touch the water - and let it remind you that you are God's beloved forgiven child." Clare had sat in the back this time, so she saw people go up throughout the service - putting their fingertips - or sometimes their whole hand in the water. Her shyness and the tears in her eyes made her want to sit still - but her sense that she needed a new beginning got her on her feet. She stood by the water and did something she hadn't done in a long time. She prayed. She prayed that she could forgive, and heal, and begin again. And she touched the water - and then touched her own forehead - as if she was blessing herself.

She turned around - and was surprised to see Susan from Shepherd's Center standing behind her. Susan put her hand on

Clare's shoulder, in a gesture that felt like reassurance - and then moved forward to touch the water for herself.

After the service ended, and the Pastor, as he always did, told them to go back out into the world, Clare waited in the back for Susan.

"I'm glad you came!" Susan said.

"I've come before - I like this service. It's different."

"I usually go in the morning, but we were away, so I thought I'd try coming at night - and it was just perfect for me. I think I'll be back."

Clare left feeling both more peaceful and more hopeful then when she'd gone in. She felt ready now - for whatever would come next.

Pete met her at her desk early on Monday morning. "I've got more good news. Tomorrow, I'm sending you to the symphony. You're becoming my non-profit specialist."

Clare realized she was really grateful for this new client. She'd come to the conclusion that working out of the office with people who cared deeply about what they were doing was the best part of her job.

Comparatively speaking, the week at the symphony was easy. The bookkeeper was totally organized, and even had ready what he thought Clare might want before she even asked for it. When it was time for Thursday, and Clare's Manna House shift — she was surprised that the week had gone by so fast.

On the way over, she found herself wondering about Paul McClain, and got so lost in her own curiosity, playing out the scenarios that might happen if a new director came aboard, she almost didn't see Gus sitting out front on the porch.

"Hey Clare," he said.

"Hi Gus. How's it going today?"

"Pretty good. The leg is almost healed, and I've had a pretty good day. You know Harvey?"

"Of course. Harvey with the blue bag."

"Yup, that's him. He does like that blue bag." Gus laughed. "Today, Harvey did a job for some people, and they paid him, and he bought muffins and shared them with everybody on the corner. It felt kind of like a party."

"That's awesome!" Clare often wondered what the guests' days were like. For Gus to describe the afternoon as feeling like a party - that was comforting to hear. Turning to go, she said, "In a few more minutes, let's hope you'll have a good dinner too."

Clare couldn't have been inside ten minutes when she noticed noise coming from the front of the building. She went out to see what was happening, and found a crowd gathered around someone on the ground. "What's going on?" she yelled.

"It's Gus," Velma yelled. "He was sitting with Harvey, up by the door. One minute he seemed fine, the next minute he's acting like he can't breathe, and then he just passes out. I yelled for help, and that lady over there called 911."

People let Clare through to where Gus was laying on the ground. She kneeled down, and took his hand, which was cold. His skin was kind of gray, but he did seem to be breathing.

The paramedics ran from the ambulance. "Anybody know what happened?"

"He was fine ten minutes ago – the people who saw it said he acted like he couldn't breathe and passed out." One of the two started taking Gus' vital signs, while the other kept asking questions.

"Who was close to him when it happened?"

Harvey was still sitting on the stoop. He wasn't making any noise, but tears were streaming down his face.

"Harvey – these men need you to help them with Gus." He nodded.

The paramedic approached Harvey. "Sir, what was happening right before he passed out?  Did he grab his chest, or say anything hurt?"

"No. Nothing like that. He was just sitting there eating the rest of my muffin."

"What kind of muffin was it?"

"Banana nut."

The paramedic pulled something out of his pocket and ran over to Gus. He talked to the other emergency worker, then he plunged a needle into Gus. The crowd got even more frightened at the sight of the needle. But then, less than a minute later, Gus seemed to stir.

"What was that?" Clare asked.

"A shot of Benadryl. His symptoms are consistent with an allergy attack, and nuts are a huge allergen."

Gus was stirring, seeing everyone staring at him, and looking afraid. Clare went to him, trying to keep him from getting up too fast. "Gus, It's me Clare. You're okay. You're right outside Manna House, and people are here taking care of you."

She turned to the paramedics. "Are you going to take him to the hospital?"

"Yes – we need to make sure there isn't something else wrong."

She looked back at Gus, at the fear in his eyes. She looked around to see if anyone he was friendly with was close by. Harvey had disappeared. He probably felt guilty – Clare made a mental note to make sure he knew that this wasn't his fault at all. Velma was gone too, now that the authorities were here.

"Clare – please – don't let them take me away." Gus's voice was garbled; he probably had a swollen tongue. He sounded scared. Just then she heard a voice behind her.

"Why don't you go with him?" Paul McClain was standing behind her. His eyes told her he'd taken in the whole situation.

"Who will run the dinner shift if I take him?"

"I'll do it. I don't know where everything is, but I'll figure it out, or somebody will help me." Clare must have still looked uncertain, because he smiled and said, "Really, it will be okay. This man - Gus is it? He seems like he needs you."

The paramedics were ready to take Gus, but Gus wouldn't let go of her hand. Clare made her decision.

"Gus – I'll follow the ambulance to the hospital. I promise." She turned to thank Paul McClain. He just nodded and motioned for her to go. She gave him the keys – which felt somehow symbolic. It occurred to her that she didn't even know for sure what he was doing there – but she trusted him. Plus, Gus needed her, and she really wanted to be there for him, the way he was always there for everybody else.

She followed the ambulance to Sarasota Hospital, and got to the Emergency Room while Gus was still answering questions. Right away she realized that the system wasn't built for people like Gus. Address – none. Phone number – none. Insurance – none. Gus started to close his eyes, as much from not having it in him to answer the questions, as from feeling sick.

"I know him, if that helps at all. His name is Gus Anderson. He lives on the East side of town, and he spends a lot of his day at 45 Manchester Drive, (which was the Manna House address.)"

"Okay. We'll put that down as an address – better something than nothing on the form."

Better something than nothing in reality – not just on the form. That's when the idea hit her. Right that minute.

All those people who ate at Manna House. Some of them couldn't work for a variety of reasons, like mental illness, or addiction, or lack of documentation. But some of them could. What did those people put on their job applications? How do you get a job, if you don't have an address? How do they tell you that they want to hire you, if you don't have a phone? What if Manna House became a place people could count on to give them their mail and their messages - the way they counted on it now as a place to eat dinner?

"Clare?" Gus spoke with his eyes still closed.

"I'm right here Gus. How are you feeling?"

"Better. Thanks. Thanks for coming. Somebody gonna get dinner on the table?"

"Absolutely. Don't worry. Everything's under control."

"Clare, please don't let them take me."

"Take you where Gus?" He closed his eyes, and she could tell by his breathing that he was asleep. What was he afraid of? She wasn't sure, but she knew she was right where she needed to be.

As he began to sleep – Clare took a pencil from her bag and began to write down her idea for Manna House. Whatever came next – she didn't want to forget what felt like an inspiration.

# Chapter 18

Gus slept hard for a while. Even when they came in to check on him, he didn't really wake up. Given his distaste for staying in shelters, Clare wondered when the last time he'd slept in a bed had been. Eventually a nurse came by and said they'd be giving him a room, because they were still worried about his breathing pattern and his blood pressure. Pulling out what were probably medical history forms, the nurse asked, "Are you his daughter?"

"No. I'm just a friend. And I'm afraid I can't help much with those. I don't really know much about Gus' health." Actually, she didn't know much about Gus period. Was there someone she should be calling?   Maybe this was a good time to try to make contact with family, if there was any? Clare decided to ask Gus, when he woke up.

"All right. I'll let him sleep for a little bit more. I'll do the next patient who just came in. But next time I come in, I'll have to wake him up. I need this information." The nurse left. She looked curious, but she was too professional to ask any more questions.

A few minutes after the nurse left, Gus started to stir. Clare, trying to keep her tone light, said, "Finally - I thought you'd never wake up. There are people around here who want to talk to you, ya know."

He slowly opened, then closed his eyes, but his mouth smiled a little. "Thanks for being here Clare. Really."

"The nurse wants to know about your medical history."

"Uh huh."

"Do you know your medical history?"

"Yes. I remember."

She kept going. "I was thinking maybe there's someone you want me to call. Somebody who might have medical records."

"No." Gus shook his head.

"No – there's nobody, or No – you don't want to call."

"Just no."   And he closed his eyes. The door to whatever went before in his life was closed, and he definitely wasn't opening it tonight.

"I'll get the nurse – before you go back to sleep."

"Isn't that what this button is for?"  Gus pushed the button beside him, and the nurses' station answered. He told them he was ready for their papers. She got up, not wanting to invade his privacy. "Where are you going?" Gus asked.

"Just in the hallway – while you talk to the nurses."

"You can stay. That way if I'm asleep, you can tell the people what they want to know."

She could feel that the real reason Gus asked her to stay was because he was afraid. But - afraid of what?

"So," said the nurse, as she walked in with her clipboard. "Looks like we've got some allergies – would that be right Mr....?"

"Andrews. August Andrews. And you can call me Gus. And no, no allergies that I know about."

"Well – they can come on you kind of out of the blue – and it definitely looks like a pretty serious nut allergy that got you tonight. You aren't aware of any other allergies then?"

"Penicillin – I remember they said I was allergic to that when I was a kid. Got hives all over me."

"That's good to know. Anything else that you know of? Do you ever eat fish?  Some people have a problem with that."

"No – no fish."

Clare said, "What about tuna?  We have tuna sometimes Gus."

"You don't have a problem with tuna?" the nurse asked.

"No – no problem with peanut butter either."

The nurse wrote all of this down and noted the vital sign numbers on the machine Gus was hooked up to. By the time she was done, Gus was almost asleep again.

The nurse told her where to get some food to bring back to the room. Clare waited until Gus was asleep and then realizing she was starving, she went down to the cafeteria, and got a sandwich and a banana. Coming back, from a distance she could see someone standing by Gus' room. As she got closer, she recognized Paul McClain.

"Hi." Clare said.

"Hi. I just wanted to stop by and see how Gus was doing."

"He's okay. They want to keep him overnight to make sure that nothing else is going on. I think his blood pressure is a little high. It's not like living on the streets is good for your health – I suppose."

Paul nodded. "Are you going home then?"

"No. Gus seems to get really scared whenever he thinks I'm leaving. I get the feeling something bad has happened to him at a hospital before, or maybe when he's been sick. I don't know. All I know is, it seems like I should be here when he wakes up."

"That's really nice of you."

She waved off his comment – to her it didn't seem like a big deal. Gus needed somebody – and she could be somebody for him. Then she remembered Manna House, which she honestly hadn't thought much about since she got in her car to follow the ambulance. "It was nice of you to do dinner at Manna House, so that I could go with Gus. How did it go?"

"Well – the posters on the wall were helpful – and I got somebody who seemed like they knew what they were doing to set-up the dining room – but apparently the meat loaf was – well – let's just say people were eating it, but they weren't smiling."

"Didn't the group who donated it tell you how long to cook it for?"

"Yes – but unfortunately – I misread the note, and warmed it up for 30 minutes at 250, instead of 20 minutes. It wasn't burned – but it wasn't real tender either."

"Oh – I'm sorry."

"Don't be sorry for me – I just felt bad for the people who'd been looking forward to it. Luckily the bread was delicious, and the salad was really good. And believe me, both of those were totally gone by the end of the night."

There was a pause in the conversation – and Clare decided it was okay to jump into the topic she was curious about. "So – what were you doing there anyway? Do you have some kind of superpower that brings you to a place just when people need you?"

"That would be nice – although when I played the superpower game as a kid, I always opted for invisibility." She laughed but didn't let him get away with that answer. It was hard enough on her curiosity to be quiet when Gus didn't tell her the things she wanted to know. She wasn't going to let this guy off the hook without a little more of a fight.

"So - why were you there? Is it a secret?"

"No. It's not a secret. I was there because I wanted to look around one more time before I gave them a final answer about the director job. And

I came on Thursday night, because I wanted to take a look around while you were in charge."

"Well you certainly got a first-hand view – although we've never had a night like that before, at least since I've been here."

"The view was good – really good. And watching the way you were with Gus, it told me what I needed to know."

"Which was..."

"I needed to know that Manna House was about more than people thinking they were doing their duty. I've seen that too many times. People providing food for people that don't have any out of guilt but looking down on the people at the same time. I needed to know that real connections were happening – that relationships were part of the deal at Manna House. And you showed me that – in as real a way as you possibly could."

"So, does that mean you are taking the job?"

"Yes. Are you glad?"

She smiled – "Well, I never met whoever your competition might have been, but yeah, I think you're all right."

"Gee thanks. Why do I feel like that's quite a compliment, coming from you?"

This guy made her laugh – which was a trait she could get used to. Clare suddenly realized there wasn't nearly enough laughter in her life.

"Do you want to see Gus?  I'm not sure if he's awake or not."

"No – he doesn't really know me. I don't want to add to his stress." He stood for a moment, as if he was deciding what to say next, and then he said, "I guess I should go."

"I do want to get back inside in case Gus wakes up."

"Yeah – and you should eat that food. Hospital food doesn't typically get better with age."

"Thanks for reminding me."  She paused, and then asked, "So, I'll be seeing you at Manna House then?"

"Yes. Once I start for real, I'm going to put a meeting together, so that I can figure out what my role really needs to be. That's the fun part of having a job no one has had before. I get to pretty much make-up the job description."

"That does sound like fun – now you're making me jealous." A noise came from Gus' room, and so Clare turned to go in, saying "Thanks again for covering for me."

"Any time – any time."

# Chapter 19

She slept on a chair in Gus' room – and about halfway through the night woke up with a start, remembering that the next day was Friday, not the weekend. What was she going to do in the morning? Call in sick to work, leave Gus for the day – she didn't know what to do. As often happened to her, nighttime thinking didn't produce any solutions. In the morning, she remembered that her contract had personal days in it - and this fit that description pretty well. She called Pete, told him a friend was in the hospital and needed her, and he said okay. He wasn't thrilled with the idea that he would have to call the symphony, so she offered to make the call from the hospital herself. She hung up from Pete, wondering what he would think if he knew the friend that needed her was a homeless man, who had to be twice her age.

Gus woke up and looked at her with sad eyes.

"What's wrong?" She asked.

"In a little while, somebody is going to come in here, and tell me I can go home. They'll want to know what home I'm going to, to make sure I'll be all right. If you tell them the truth – they'll send me to a state facility."

"And that's bad? Is that what you've been acting so scared about? Have you been there before?"

Gus nodded. "One other time. I told them I didn't have a place to go, I thought they'd send me to a place with a bed to sleep in, and that would be good, because I didn't feel like I was ready to sleep on the ground. But it was a terrible place. No doorknobs on the doors, bars on the windows. They kept asking me questions. Finally – I figured out if I wanted to get out, I had to answer their questions the way they wanted me to. I don't want to go back there – ever."

It was the most Gus had ever said about himself. She thought about what he was saying and realized that she'd already given them an address for him. She'd given them Manna House, just because she didn't know what else to say. So, he might not get the third degree, because whoever was on duty now wouldn't know that she'd said he spends his time there, not that he lives there. But was Gus ready to just get out of here and go back to life on the street?

The nurse came in – sure enough a different one from the night before. "Good morning. Did you sleep all right?"

Gus nodded yes, while she started hooking him up to the blood pressure machine and something that measured his blood oxygen level.

"Your pressure looks much better this morning. And your oxygen level is 98. I think the Doctor is going to be pleased with you." She left, and Gus and Clare looked at each other.

"Gus, I already gave them Manna House when they asked me for your address last night. I don't think they'll ask you that many questions about whether you can handle life at home. Why were you in the last time?"

"I broke my ankle. In a fight – I wasn't in it, but the two guys started pushing each other, and one of them fell into me, bent my ankle all the way over."

"Well then, maybe they asked you all those questions because they wanted to know if you could get around with a broken ankle."

"All I know is, I told them, I lived on the street, and the next thing I know I was in this place - I don't even know its name. I used to, but I tried to erase my memory." Gus' hands were beginning to shake.

"Okay – let's not get your blood pressure going up. We want you to be getting better, okay?"

Gus nodded, but he still looked distraught. "Gus – if they won't just release you – what if I sign for you?" Clare heard herself saying it – without having consciously thought it first. The ever-present voice in her head was ahead of her this morning.

"You would do that?"

"Well – I'd do it if you agreed to go someplace safe that I find for you. You can't just sleep on the street. I agree with the doctors and nurses about that."

"Why not? It's not like sleeping on the street makes me more likely to eat nuts. I get it – I'm allergic to nuts now. I can't just eat what I want. I won't do it again. Isn't that good enough for you people?" Gus' voice rose. It hit her that he wanted to be in control – just like everybody else she knew.

The nurse came in, saying, "Your doctor is on his way in — and he'll probably release you." She turned to her, saying, "Will you be driving him home?"

And that easily, Clare just said, "Yes." They didn't ask any of the questions Gus feared — and she didn't volunteer information that they probably would have wanted. Clare didn't think what she did was illegal — but it did feel a little unethical. Still — it was clear that Gus wouldn't thrive in a system that thought he was crazy because he lived on the street.

The nurse left, and Gus relaxed back into his pillow. "Thank you. Better get some sleep while I still have a bed with a mattress and a pillow. Don't want to take this for granted." And he was asleep within minutes. Clare, on the other hand, was wide-awake, trying to figure out what she was going to do next.

# Chapter 20

Okay – point one – Gus was not crazy. Clare totally believed that. Point two – Gus was not ready to sleep on the street. She believed that, although he wouldn't agree. She considered for a moment whether she would ever think Gus was ready to sleep on the street. The answer was no. So – if the answer's no, was she wrong thinking he shouldn't go back to the street right now? Was it just her bias in favor of what she thought should be best for Gus coming out?

He didn't like shelters. She knew that. He said they weren't as safe as the streets – which made no sense to her – but she had to trust him, since she had no first-hand experience. He did like beds - clearly. He was run down, he needed more recovery time than the hospital system could give him. At least until the bumps and bruises from where he fell when he passed out healed enough for him to be able to rest somewhere that wasn't soft and cushioned.

A thought began to formulate in her brain. She let it roll around a little in there, before she let the words come out of her mouth, even if she was the only one that could hear them. "I could take him home. I have a spare room. He could stay there, at least for a day or two."

When she heard herself say it - it seemed like a perfectly reasonable idea. But then she could imagine her family's voices talking back to her. "You have no clue who he really is. You don't know his background. What if he robs you or worse? You're the one that's crazy for even thinking of a plan like this." Kate would definitely think the voice in her head was driving her around the bend - right past brave and on to reckless.

Which reminded her – she needed to call the Symphony – before they called the office to say she wasn't there. She got the number out of her bag, and reached the bookkeeper, Sam on the first ring.

"Sam, this is Clare. I just wanted you to know I'm not going to be in today. I've got a friend in the hospital, who needs me to take him home."

"Oh – I'm sorry about your friend. Is there anything I can do?"

It would have seemed like an odd remark, but not coming from Sam. Clare'd noticed that he had a compassionate personality. "No – I'm okay. I've got it figured out."  And saying those words, Clare realized she did have it figured out, no matter what anyone else thought. "Thanks though. I'll see you on Monday, okay?"

"Sure. See you then."

She looked down at Gus sleeping. Answering the imagined concerns of her family, Clare thought, 'I do know him – maybe not in the informational vital statistics way, but in the more real way. He's a person, with a good heart, who always looks out for everybody else. This time, he's the one who needs help. And I'm the one that's here.'

Just then, the Doctor came in. He looked at Gus' vitals and nodded his head that they were acceptable. Then he began to examine Gus, and said, "I think overall, you're going to be fine, but these bruises are pretty bad. Did you fall during your allergy attack?"

"Not far - but yeah, I guess I did fall. I'm fine though - nothing broken or anything."

"Okay, well even without anything broken you're going to have some pain for a few days. Stay off your feet, let your body heal, okay?"

The Doctor smiled at Gus, expecting him to nod, which he did. Then he signed something and left to tell the nurse Gus was ready to be released.

The nurse came back in and set the forms on the table for Gus to sign. "Sir, I need you to fill these out, so we can get you out of here." She left to answer someone else's buzz.

Emboldened by the Doctor's words Clare spoke. "You know Gus, the Doctor just said you need to stay off your feet, which is pretty much impossible if you're on the street. Why don't you stay at my house for a few nights?  I think it might help you get back to your regular life sooner, if you had a few more nights of sleep in a bed."

"You have a house?"

"Well – an apartment – with an extra bedroom. It's not far from Manna House."

"I can't do that. Thanks – but I can't do that."

"Why can't you do that?"

"You don't want me in your home."

"Why don't I want you in my home?"

"Because - people don't want people in their homes that live on the street. It's just the way it is. You know that Clare."

"What if I don't like to do things the way other people do them? What if I don't want to do what everybody else does? You keep telling me you don't like to go places people want you to go – do things people want you to do. I'm like you. I don't like to do what other people tell me to do." As she was saying this she realized that lots of times, she was a people pleaser. With Danny, she'd always done whatever she could to make him happy, even to the point of telling herself she was happy when she wasn't. But maybe now she was also becoming a little bit of a risk-taker. That was an idea that appealed to her. "Listen Gus, I vouched for you – I need to feel like that wasn't a lie."

"Okay, okay. Relax. If you are this set on this idea, I guess I could stay at your apartment for a night."

She didn't push for more than that. One day at a time seemed like a good way to live out this situation.

# Chapter 21

Taking Gus home, he sat in the front seat of her car, and got really jumpy. Finally, Clare asked, "What's the matter? Don't you like my driving?"

"Truth is – I don't ride in cars much. Can't remember the last time. Buses – sure. But not cars. Feels so small and low to the ground. I feel like everybody is going to run right over us."

"My car is particularly small – which probably isn't helping. But it gets great gas mileage, and with the price of gas at almost $3 a gallon – that matters." She could tell by the look on Gus' face that the gas price surprised him too. Which made sense - If you don't drive, why would you pay attention to those details?

They got to the apartment, and she took Gus to his room, gave him sheets and pillows and blankets for his bed. It was lunchtime, so she went to warm up some soup – the only lunch kind of food she had in the house.

She looked in from the kitchen, and saw Gus looking at one of the prints on the wall. It was actually a good one – a serigraph she bought from an art auction for charity that one of her clients had.

"That's France." Gus said it as a statement, not a question.

"Yes – Delacroix paints French scenes – he's one of my favorites."

Gus kept staring at the painting. Finally, he said, "It looks like that. Not exactly, but close. Right before sunset in front of Notre Dame, it looks like that."

"I've never been there. I want to go, someday."

"You should. You'd like it."

She couldn't keep herself from asking, "When did you go to France?"

"I lived there. When I was just about your age. I was twenty-two and I moved to France. I wanted to be a writer, and I was convinced that writers should live in Paris."

Gus – a writer. That wasn't something she would have guessed. But why not? He was articulate, intelligent. Was it possible that even after her experiences at Manna House, she still thought of homeless people as if they didn't have any successes in life before they ended up on the street?

Gus seemed ready to talk about this part of his life, so she kept going with her questions. "And did it work?  Were you able to write in Paris?"

"I lived in Paris for two years – and I didn't write a thing. Too much to see, too many distractions. My Dad had given me an allowance – but that ran out, and I had to come home."

"Your Dad supported you being a writer in Paris?  That's pretty cool."

Gus looked at her and shook his head. "My Dad supported me moving to Paris, because it suited him. He'd just married his third wife, and he didn't want me around as a reminder of how old he really was. Writing a check was always the way my Dad was part of my life."

"Well, writing a check is better than nothing I guess." Clare offered this out of her own need to make good out of bad – but Gus didn't accept it.

"No – it wasn't better. It fooled me for a long time. I expected love to be behind the money, and when it wasn't it hurt pretty bad."  Suddenly realizing how forthcoming he'd been, Gus stopped himself, saying, "But that was all a really long time ago. Doesn't matter now. So - what's that smell?"

"Campbell's healthy choices – Italian Wedding Soup. Is that okay?"

"Clare – I'm used to accepting whatever anybody makes, remember?"

Funny, she had forgotten for a minute. "Okay – I see your point – but do you like it?  For the record, your other choices are peanut butter and jelly sandwiches, or a bowl of Shredded Wheat."

"Soup – definitely soup."

Clare went out to the kitchen, and Gus followed her. They set the table – the one she only ate at when visitors came to town. As much as it felt wrong to just eat in front of the television – she couldn't quite get used to having dinner without conversation. Too many years of family dinners. The people on the T.V. filled in the gaps.

They sat down to what wasn't half bad soup. "So – you wanted to be a writer."

"I was a writer – in a way."

"I thought you said you didn't write anything."

"I said I didn't write anything in Paris. I wrote for a few years when I got back home."

"What did you write?"

"News. I worked for a local paper. It wasn't the novel I thought about when I was a kid, but it was okay for a while. What about you, what do you do for work?"

"I'm an accountant."

"Do you like doing that?"

"Lately, I like it more. I've been getting to go out to different clients. It's like getting a glimpse of different people's worlds. I like that. When I was a kid, I wanted to work for the United Nations. I wanted to know all the languages, and help people talk to each other. In some ways – learning the language of how money works is like knowing a universal language. I'd still rather work for world peace – but this isn't so bad."

Gus smiled. "Yup – I know what you mean. Writing for the paper made me feel connected to other people's stories too."

"So, do you ever write now Gus?"

He shook his head. "No."

"You know – I think a lot of people would want to read about your life now."

"Who?"

"Well – the people who volunteer at Manna House for starters. I think a lot of us would like to have a picture of what life is like for you and for the other people who live on the street. What if we made a Manna House newspaper?  Or maybe a Street Life newspaper. I don't know what to call it, but the point is I bet there are lots of stories that need telling, and if we put them together in one place, people might be interested in reading them."

"You do realize that life on the street doesn't have a lot of happy endings."

"I know – but I think people would want to hear your voice and hear other people's voices."

"Who?  The tourists that try to pretend we don't exist? The police who keep asking us to move on, so that the tourists won't know we exist?  Maybe the business people, who want to make sure we aren't on their doorstep when they come in in the morning, because they want the tourists to shop at their store?"

"Okay - those are fair points. Maybe I have to think this out a little. I'm not saying I agree with you — I just don't have a whole plan yet."

Gus smiled at her, like he was the indulgent uncle, and she was the zany niece. It felt odd - like a tide change in their relationship. Maybe because at Manna House, she was the authority. Plus, at Manna House, Gus never talked like this, never got into these kinds of discussions. Other people did, but not Gus. Gus was telling her more about his life, but the more he told her, the less she understood.

# Chapter 22

Gus slept most of the rest of Friday, clear into late Saturday morning. At lunchtime, he started making noise about wanting to get up and out, but she reminded him that it was the weekend, and he'd told her himself that the weekends were the most stressful time to be on the street. They sat for a while and watched television – mostly sports –, which was fine with Clare.

Clare anticipated her parent's weekly call with some level of distress. They always called around 2:00 on Saturday. They seemed to think that was a good time, because of their delusion that she went out on Saturday nights. When the phone rang, Clare went into her bedroom to talk.

"Hey Clare. How's the weather today?" Since she moved to Florida, her Dad always started conversations like that. Clare got the feeling he was proud of her for moving out of the cold.

"It's good Dad. Really good. 80 degrees, and a nice breeze."

"Wish I was there."

"Well, come and visit."

"Your Mother and I were talking about it. Spring break isn't too far away, and I was thinking maybe we could come down." Clare's Dad was an English teacher. He could get kids excited about reading anything. His classes always filled up, and from what all of her friends said, she definitely got the short end of the stick, when she had to take someone else for English Lit sophomore year.

"I'd love to see you guys. And I'd love to show you around. I've figured out a lot about this area since you helped me move in. I could be a good tour guide now."

"Okay honey, that sounds great. Your Mom wants me to put her on now. I'll talk to you later."

"Bye Dad."

"Hi Clare. How's your week been?"

Her Mom tended to ask more questions. She knew that this conversation was going to require a decision about what she was going to share – and then the strength to stick to it.

"It was a good week Mom. I got to go out again, this time to symphony hall."

"That's great that they are sending you out on jobs to so many interesting places. I'm proud of you sweetheart. That must mean you are doing well."

"I think so. It was a fascinating place. Yo-Yo Ma played there last year." That would definitely interest her Mom. Though she hadn't been sure what to say about Gus, as soon as she heard her Mom's voice, she knew that she didn't want to make her worry. Knowing her, she'd be liable to jump in the car and make the twenty-hour trip down, just to make sure she was okay.

They talked for a few minutes and were about to hang up when Clare's Mom said, "Are you watching tennis?  I thought you hated watching tennis. You said it was like a form of torture when I tried to get you to watch it with me."

The game they'd been watching must have ended. Clearly the sound of tennis was in the background. Clare felt like she'd been caught doing something wrong. "I thought I'd give it one more try, just for you Mom. Sorry - still don't like it. Well, I've got to run. I'll talk to you later." She got off quickly, afraid that if her Mom sensed something off, she'd be relentless with her questions.

Looking around the kitchen, Clare saw there was absolutely nothing for dinner. A trip to the store was called for, and maybe that was a good thing. It would give Clare a chance to get out of the apartment and give Gus a chance to have the space for himself for a little while. She wondered when the last time Gus had privacy was. One thing she wasn't worried about was him taking anything. She would have bet anything he'd never steal from her, or anyone else for that matter.

"Gus – I need to go pick up some food. Do you think you'd be okay for about an hour or so?"

"You're going to leave me here?" Gus seemed very nervous at the idea.

"I'm sorry. Don't you feel well?  I can stay."

"No – I'm fine. I'm just – are you sure you want to leave me in your apartment by myself?"  Now he was making Clare nervous.

"Gus, is there some reason why I shouldn't leave you in my apartment by yourself?"

"It's pretty crazy that you invited me into your apartment, if you think about it. You don't know me that well. Now you want to leave me alone with your stuff?"

He was wrong about the order of things she was worried about. Clare really didn't think he'd take anything, and if he did, she'd be more upset about the fact that she'd been such a bad judge of character than anything else. Face it - what stuff did she have that wasn't replaceable?  The ability to trust her own sixth sense about people – that would be irreplaceable.

"Listen Gus, if you steal from me that would be your choice. Trusting you is my choice. Besides, why would you steal something from me?  If you want something, you could just ask me, and I'd probably give it to you anyway."

Gus sat looking at her for a while, trying to take in what she was saying. He began to smile, slowly, first his lips and then his eyes. "Thanks Clare. I'll be fine here. Go ahead and do whatever you want to do."

So, she left – shopped for the makings of Pasta Bolognese, her best dish, and was back home in less than an hour.

Driving home, she was at peace about how the weekend was going until she got to her apartment, and Gus didn't answer the door. She found her keys, unlocked the door, half-afraid she'd find Gus on the floor. Instead, she found a note on the kitchen table.

"Thanks for everything Clare. I appreciate it. It's time for me to leave now. Gus"

Funny, when she was thinking about how Gus might enjoy time to himself, it never occurred to her that he would leave. But maybe it did make sense. He felt uncomfortable in her space; he didn't want to put her out. In his own way, he wanted to go home.

Judging by the dishes in the sink, at least he ate a sandwich before he left, which was good. But now what? Should she do something?  What could she do?  He seemed to be past the crisis, and at least he'd had a few good nights of sleep, between the hospital and her house. Still, she couldn't just sit in her apartment. She picked up her keys and left the apartment, without a plan.

# Chapter 23

Almost automatically, Clare's car drove itself over to Manna House. Even after it was closed, people often hung around talking out front. It was a pretty nice evening, not too hot. She pulled in the driveway and saw some of the regulars. Maria was there with her kids, and Velma. And she was happy to see that Tom was back too - talking with the others as if he was trying to fit in. As she pulled up, the kids recognized her and ran to her car.

"Clare, we missed you this week. Where were you?" They must not have been in the area when Gus was taken to the hospital, which was a good thing. The ambulance would have scared them. Even if they'd been there, Maria would have whisked them all away when an authority figure showed up.

"Gus was sick, but he's a lot better now." Paul McClain came out the door as she was talking.

Clare said, "You're here again?  I thought it would be awhile before you started actually working here. Don't you have to give notice some place?"

"Actually, I gave notice to my job awhile ago. My last job kept me too busy to even apply for anything else. I needed to be free to concentrate on finding a job like this one."

"Wow!  Quitting a job without another one already in the pocket. My Midwestern parents would have had a lot of trouble with that."

"Yeah – well my Florida parents weren't so hot on the idea either, but sometimes you just know you've got to do what you've got to do. Know what I mean?"

Clare nodded yes, remembering the voice in her head that gave her that kind of courage, on rare occasions.

"So, I heard you say Gus was doing better?  That's great. Did he get out of the hospital?  Where is he?"

"Yes – he got out yesterday."  She paused, not wanting to say too much in front of the kids. But they were already bouncing off to play again with Velma and their Mom. "He went home with me, but he left when I went out. I think he's okay, he had his color back, but I just feel funny having him back on the street so soon."

"You took him home with you?  You are an interesting woman Clare Wheeler."

Clare could feel her cheeks get red. "It wasn't a big deal. Really. Gus was easy to have around."

Paul kept looking at her, and she began to be uncomfortable. "What?  What are you thinking?"

"I'm just thinking that I don't know anybody male or female who invites a stranger off the street to stay with them. Truthfully, I don't know anybody who would have even considered the idea. What makes you so different?"

How do you answer a question like that? "First of all, Gus isn't a stranger. And you know what else -the people you know don't know Gus. And the people you know didn't hear the fear in his voice, when he thought they might send him to an inpatient ward if he didn't have a place to go. Not that he asked to come home with me. What he really wanted me to do was pretend he had an address to go to and help him get out of the hospital. I wanted him to go to a home with a bed, not just pretend to go. But anyway, he's gone now."

"Sounded like you thought he was okay though, right?"

"Yes. He was fine. I think he felt ready to go home. No matter what I think about it, he has his own notion of home. I guess I just needed to talk out loud about it, to feel better that he left while I was gone." Suddenly, Clare remembered the thoughts she'd had in the hospital about people needing an address. It clicked into her mind that now that Manna House had a director, it might be a real possibility. "This conversation is reminding me of an idea I had, while I was with Gus in the hospital. If you're on board as the new director, maybe you'd like to hear it?"

"I'd definitely like to hear it. Let's make a time when we could meet for lunch and talk about it."

"Oh, I could tell you anytime – it wouldn't take that long."

"Too bad – I was hoping to use it as an excuse."

"An excuse?"

"An excuse to ask you out, without having to risk a rejection."

"What?"  She didn't get what he was saying at first – and then she did. "Oh – Yes – Yes – let's talk about it at lunch."  Clare hoped that the red on her cheeks wasn't too obvious in the dimming sunlight. Paul McClain was definitely smoother than she was.

He smiled at her, then said, "You know what – if you're not doing anything now, I'd love to hear about your idea tonight. I was so busy getting to know folks during the dinner hour, I forgot to eat."

"Truth is, I'm pretty hungry too. I left my apartment without eating." That was better – casual acceptance of what was a pretty casual invitation.

"Should we take my car?"

She smiled. "I guess that would be okay. I mean how many times do you know the person you're about to get in a car with had to pass a background check in the last month to get his job?"

Paul laughed, saying "Okay then! How do you feel about Indian food?"

"How do you know where there's an Indian food restaurant? You've been in this town for like a minute and a half."

"It's one of the first things I look for when I come into a community. I have to know where the interesting restaurants are. Since I'm not much of a cook – that's pretty much a survival issue for me. It helps me figure out where I want to live. So, would you like to try the Indian place?"

"Sure! I love Indian food."

They found the restaurant pretty quickly. The lights were down a little low but overall the ambiance was nice - felt a little like they'd moved into another country, and she liked the Indian music playing softly in the background. On the other hand, all of that made it harder to act like this wasn't a date. Pretending this was just a casual evening was what she was counting on to make her less nervous. She decided to start the conversation that had begun this whole experience.

"So, I had this idea."

"Right – the idea. Tell me about it."

"Well, when I was in the hospital with Gus, and they asked for his address, I thought about how hard it must be for people who are on the street to try to find a job. I mean, I know some people on the street aren't employable, but some could be, and yet if they go to fill out a job application, what do they put for their address? And what do they put as a phone number? Or an e-mail?

Well, maybe they have one of those, and they could check it at the library or something – but still – do you see what I'm saying?"

"I think so. You're saying that feeding people is good – but we could do more." Clare was impressed by how quickly he'd been able to say "we" about the job that he'd just started. She still struggled with thinking of herself as part of her company!

"Yes. I'm saying Manna House could be more for people. You'll figure out, if you haven't yet, that it already is much more than a place for people to eat. It's like their home base – they know they'll be there everyday. They know they'll see familiar faces everyday. It just makes sense to me that Manna House could be a place whose address and phone number they put as their home." She realized her excitement was rising as she talked – and stopped herself. "So, what do you think?"

"I like it. It needs some strategic planning, board approval, procedural steps. But, I like it. And I like hearing you talk about it."

This man made Clare's cheeks turn red more often than she was comfortable with.

"Okay – now you talk for awhile."

"What about?"

"Well, for example, tell me what you didn't want to tell me that day we met at the bookstore. What have you been doing before you came here?"

"I worked at a YMCA up in Brandon, not too far from Tampa."

"What did you do there?"

"I directed their programs, made schedules, figured out what families might want to do. I trained and hired people to work with their climbing wall, teach swimming lessons, whatever we thought people needed we tried to provide."

"Sounds busy."

"Really busy. Very little off time, lots of crises – that aren't actually crises, but they feel like crises, because there's somebody loudly complaining about something. And then sometimes there are real crises – like somebody getting hurt, or a child getting left."

"A child getting left? What does that mean?"

"Yeah – that's the thing that happened that really got me thinking about where I felt like I wanted to spend my time. This kid, three years old. His mom dropped him off in the exercise center playroom, and she didn't come back to get him. You aren't supposed to leave the center, but she did, and we didn't have a valid cell phone on record for her. We didn't want to call the police; we kept waiting, hoping she'd come back. The workers had to leave, so I put some of my program staff in the playroom to play with him. He was such a great kid. Just when we were ready to close the Y, and we would have had to call the police, she showed up hysterical. She looked like she'd been crying for hours. I tried to calm her down before she went to see her son. She said they'd lost their apartment when her husband left them, and she'd thought he'd be better off without her. But she couldn't do it – she couldn't leave him. You should have seen his face light up when she came in to get him. He was too young to know what was happening, but he knew something was wrong. We called around to find a place for them to stay – and it wasn't easy. Finally, we found a church that would let them sleep there for the night, and then in the morning we found a social worker who said she'd help them figure out what to do next."

He stopped for a minute. Clare got the feeling he'd been reliving the story while he was telling it to her.

"After that, I didn't have much tolerance for the small stuff. Not that the small stuff wasn't important. It was important - well most of it was. And the work we did at the Y, I was proud of it. But I just had this sense that there was something else I was supposed to be doing with my life. That sounds weird - doesn't it? It's just that I've always had a feeling that there's a life that is mine to live, and I felt like I wasn't living it. So – I looked around, and I found Manna House."

"How did you find Manna House?"

"Idealist.org, believe it or not."

"There's a website called idealist.org? Seriously?"

"Yes. A friend told me about it, and the first day I looked at it, I saw the Manna House job. I turned in a resume, and well, you were there for most of the rest of the story."

He stopped talking for a minute, and the waitress, who'd apparently been keeping a discreet distance while they'd been looking busy, approached the table.

"Excuse me. Would you like to order off the menu, or do you want the buffet?"

"I'd like the buffet," Clare said immediately. "I like to try a little bit of everything."

"Sounds good to me," Paul responded.

"All right. We'll bring your naan to the table, and you can go over to the buffet whenever you're ready."

"Personally, I could just eat four courses of naan." Clare said, as they went to see what else there was.

"Yes – but if you like spicy – they've got some really good lamb vindaloo here." She had a funny feeling all of sudden, wondering how many other women Paul had brought to this place in the short time he'd been in town. Jealousy? Ridiculous – but apparently true.

"This is a first for me too. I've never eaten in the dining room here before – I've just ordered take-out, so I don't know much about this buffet. We'll be exploring it together."

Geez – did she say that thing about other women out loud, or was he really that good at reading her face that he knew what she was thinking? She decided to hope he was just talking – not in response to anything from her. The alternative was too embarrassing to contemplate.

There were at least fifteen choices on the table. Everything from salad with a yogurt dressing, to spicy lentils, to a coconut milk rice pudding. She got caught up in all the options, filling her plate to overflowing. Oh well – if dainty eater was important to this guy, it would be good for him to know that wasn't her.

As they sat down, Paul said, "Okay, now your turn to tell me what I didn't know how to tactfully ask you when we met at the book store. Aren't you a little young to have the responsibility for a whole night at Manna House?"

"I suppose. But it just happened naturally. I volunteered, they had a training session, and they put me on the list. No one asked my age."

"Well, obviously they made a good decision. If they'd thought about it, they might not have gone along with it – reverse ageism."

"I'm not sure about that. It's not like you're that old, and they put you in charge of the whole place." She was nervous for a minute that he was older than she thought.

"I'm thirty. You know how people are. Thirty is a lot older than…twenty-four?"

"Twenty-three and a half to be exact."

They talked through dinner about movies, books, and football. She'd been in Florida long enough to know they took their football very seriously. "Okay – Gator fan or Seminoles?"

"Gators, of course. I didn't go to UF, but I grew up on the Gators. My whole family - <u>huge</u> Gator fans. Once one of my cousins planned a wedding on a game day, and my Dad bought a mini T.V. that he could hide in his pocket. My Mom told him he was only allowed to watch it in the bathroom. He ended up in the bathroom for the whole last quarter, with like ten other guys gathered around watching this 2-inch screen."

"Yeah – where I grew up the U of M, Ohio State game was huge. People had more parties for that than they did for the Super Bowl. But I think it's even more intense here. If your Dad was that into it, I'm surprised you didn't just go to UF on automatic pilot."

"Well, senior year, I wasn't exactly overly identified with what my parents wanted me to do. In fact, I think I purposely left UF off my list of colleges, so I wouldn't cave to pressure at the last minute."

"So – where did you go?"

"I went up north, to a college in New Jersey."

Was it her imagination, or was he being overly secretive? What was the big deal about telling her what college he went to? A more tactful person would have probably taken the hint and changed the subject. Clearly, Clare was more curious than tactful.

"Which college in New Jersey?"

His face turned a little red, and he said, "Princeton."

"Princeton. Seriously?"

"Well, I wouldn't make that up."

"That's great." Clare looked at him with a newfound respect for his intellect.

"See that look right there. That's why I don't like to tell people. They make all kinds of assumptions when I say that, and I gotta tell you, it's really not that different from other schools."

"Okay – I won't make assumptions. You tell me what it was like, and I'll tell you if it wasn't that different from the college I went to."

"And where was that?"

"Alma College. It's in the center of Michigan. It's a pretty small school. Liberal arts for undergraduates, I was the rare person who came out with a degree in accounting."

"In some ways – Princeton felt like a liberal arts school to me. Most people get another degree after a Princeton undergrad. And Princeton isn't that big. Although I'll admit that sometimes, it felt bigger, because of all the students from all over the world. That was my favorite part of being there."

"If I had gone to Princeton, my favorite part would have been walking on the sidewalks where people have been walking and learning for centuries. I love the history. The sense that I'm part of something that started way before me."

Paul was looking at her with that funny look again. The same one he'd had on his face when she told him she brought Gus home with her "What are you thinking?" Clare asked.

"I'm thinking you say things that surprise me."

"Do you like surprises?"

"I definitely like surprises." His voice had a smile in it that made her smile.

"So, which was your favorite dish?" Clare's voice sounded deeper and breathier than usual. She felt like she was wearing a sign around her neck advertising that she was attracted to this guy.

"Will you judge me if I say my favorite dish is always dessert? I loved the rice pudding. I know we're supposed to be in the era of getting healthier, eating right, and I do eat my vegetables. But my favorite part of any meal is still the part with the sugar in it."

"Chocolate? Yay or nay." She asked.

"100% Yay."

"Thank goodness. I find it impossible to get along with anyone who doesn't agree with me that chocolate is God's gift to humanity. The darker and richer the better."

Paul was giving her a weird look again. "What are you doing?" he asked, gesturing at her glass.

Clare looked down to realize she was drawing invisible squares on the napkin with the base of her glass. It was a nervous habit, a sure sign that she was feeling out of control, but in a good way. Clare just laughed and said, "I have no idea."

Paul looked at his watch. "Do you realize its 10 o'clock?" They were the only ones left in the restaurant. "I guess we better go," he said. He sounded like he wasn't ready for the night to end, which made Clare feel a little less vulnerable about the feelings she was having.

He drove her back to Manna House and parked his car next to hers. As she started to get out, he touched her shoulder. "Thanks for coming out with me, Clare. It's great to have a new friend so soon in a new place."

The feeling Clare had when he touched her shoulder wasn't exactly what she would describe as friendship, but she went with his word. "Anytime – I'm always glad to make new friends."

Shoot – now she'd be obsessing over whether he used that word because he didn't want to take a risk letting her know he liked her, or whether he wanted her to know he was putting her in the friend category, so she wouldn't do anything embarrassing, like lean in to kiss him. Oh well, no matter what, she knew from experience that she was destined to rethink every part of their conversation all night, wondering what each word meant. At least he'd given her something concrete to focus her angst on.

She picked up the phone the moment she walked in the door. Good thing that it was never too late to call Kate. She gave her sister a play-by-play of her Indian food evening. Kate told her to stop obsessing, and just see where things went, even though she knew Clare would never be able to do that. What Clare still didn't mention was the time she spent with Danny. She just wasn't ready to talk about that - not yet - maybe not ever.

# Chapter 24

Monday morning, she was back at the Symphony and finished everything up by five. Leaving the parking lot, she couldn't decide where to go. No one expected her to go back to the office, and she just didn't feel ready to go home. She drove over to Siesta Key beach, grabbed the shorts that were in her car for just such an occasion and decided to walk in the gorgeous white sand, letting the breeze blow the cobwebs out of her brain.

The early evening was her favorite time to walk on the beach. Less crowded, no need for sunscreen as the sun was beginning to move down in the sky. It was more than breezy today. The wind was so strong that walking against it felt like a workout. A couple times, Clare felt as though it was going to pick her up.

When her cell phone rang, she almost didn't answer it; it seemed kind of sacrilegious to be on the beach and not pay full attention to how beautiful the day was. But then she saw it was Kate and wanted to hear her voice.

"Hey Kate."

"Hi Clare. Man – why is it so noisy where you are?"

"Oh – that's the wind. I'm walking on the beach."

"Are you kidding me?  I thought you told me you worked so much you barely ever got to the beach."

"I didn't say I never got to the beach."

"Well actually, I'm glad to hear you aren't such a workaholic that you are missing the good parts of living in Florida, a thousand miles from home."

"For the record, I'm not anywhere near a workaholic. You should see some of the people in my office. They come in way before I get there, and they don't even leave while the sun is out."

"Sounds like you work with some pretty intense people. Are you ready for me to come down there and get in the way of all that intensity?"

"That would be awesome!  Are you really coming?"

"Is Friday night too soon?  I have one of those awkward breaks, where the dorms are closed, but I feel too old to go sleep in my childhood bedroom. I've got some frequent flyer miles Mom and Dad gave me that I could use. What do you think?"

"Friday night would be perfect." Clare was glad she didn't say Thursday. She didn't want to miss her time at Manna House, for more reasons than she wanted to admit at the moment.

"Have you seen your new "friend" since we talked last?" Her sister the mind reader.

"No, and he hasn't called me either. But I'll probably see him on Thursday. So, you'll be getting here just in time to analyze every single thing he says and does."

"Great – can't wait. And Clare…"

"Yes?"

"For once in your life – try to stay in the moment with this guy. Just enjoy it. Please. Seriously, I'm begging you."

"Okay, okay. I'll try."

"All right. Well, enjoy your walk, and I'll see you on Friday night at the Sarasota airport. I'll e-mail you my flight info."

"I'll be there."

Clare hung up, with a smile on her face. That call had actually improved her ability to enjoy the day. Stay in the moment, Kate said. Watching the waves hit the shore, over and over again – there wasn't anywhere else she'd rather be.

# Chapter 25

The week seemed to drag by, until she got to Thursday morning, and then the pace was fast enough to keep Clare from glancing at the clock more than once an hour. She was packing up her things when Pete came by her desk and looked surprised.

"Didn't anyone tell you there's no such thing as leaving on time in the accounting world? I know you're not working the Thursday night shift - but leaving at five - that's unheard of."

"Well - I guess I'm going to be the exception that proves the rule - at least on Thursdays." Purposefully, she picked up her purse, and got her keys ready. Pete didn't really seem to know what to do with that. Clare realized she'd opened herself up for a question on what she did on Thursdays, but he didn't ask it; he just smiled and moved politely out of her way. Clare liked what she took to be his respect for her boundaries. Her night at Manna house, and the chance to see what developed with Paul was on her mind, and she didn't want to be late because of a conversation at work that would likely make very little sense to Pete, or anybody else who might overhear it.

No one was on the porch when she got there. It was too hot of a day to be out if you didn't have to be. The door was locked, and Clare felt a little disappointment at that, wondering if it was a sign that Paul wasn't there.

But as soon as she unlocked the door and went in, she could see he was around. The tables were set. The air conditioning was running, and from the kitchen she heard sounds of pots and pans.

"Hello," she called out.

"Hi Clare. I'm in here, come on back." His voice was so clear and strong. Funny how you pay more attention to someone's voice when you can't see their face.

"Before I say anything else, I want to tell you that Gus has been in for dinner every day this week. He seems to be doing just fine. The first day, he was a little bit of a celebrity, because of the way he went out of here. But now, things are moving back into their normal pace."

"I'm so relieved to hear that. I was hoping I'd get to see him tonight. I'm imagining it might be a little awkward, and I'd like to get through that."

"I think he probably will be here. And I think you'll have to be the one to decide how to handle it, cuz my guess is, he's going to pretend nothing ever happened."

"Gotcha. So, on a different but related note, how goes the new job?" She asked.

"It's fascinating. I'm working my way through the library, learning everything I can about the government grants we've gotten in addition to all the religious organizations that support us. I want to make sure I don't miss any deadlines.

"Sounds like pretty dry reading."

"Actually, it's not. In order to get grants you have to be a good storyteller. Good enough that you make people want to support what you're doing. And the people that wrote these did a great job of telling the stories of this place. What Manna House is about, how it makes a difference for people. I feel like reading it has given me a running start."

"Well, I can see you've had a running start on getting things going here." Clare was aware that she was forcing a light tone to be in her voice, but she was feeling something else. What was that feeling bubbling up?  After a few seconds thought, she knew what was wrong. She wasn't happy that he'd done so much – it felt like she was going to be just an extra person, instead of a key part of Manna House on Thursday nights. She turned toward the listing of the volunteers and meal for the night, in case what she was thinking was showing on her face.

"I was hoping if I got things going, I'd be able to have a few minutes to talk to you before we opened the doors."  At least his motivation was good.

"Well, sure. We could talk while we finish getting set-up. Let's just get the food in the ovens, and then we'll be down to mixing the lemonade and ice tea."

They moved around the kitchen together; she admitted to herself that it was actually kind of fun to be doing the work with him. "So – anything specific you wanted to talk about?"

"Actually yes. I wanted to tell you I had a really great time the other night, and I wondered if you did too, if you might want to go out again sometime."

Clare smiled. "Yes, I would like that." He must have been pretty confident that she would say yes. Otherwise, why risk how uncomfortable it would be to spend a whole evening with somebody who'd just turned you down?

"My schedule is kind of unusual – I pretty much work until 8:00 or later every night. Technically Monday is my day off, but even then, I'm on call. I don't come in until noon, so staying out late isn't bad for me – but is that too late for you? That's why I didn't just call you on the phone. I was afraid you'd think I was really strange to ask you out, but not want to pick you up until 9:00 at night." He'd worried about sounding strange. Finally – a crack in the togetherness of Paul McClain.

"The truth is, I'm pretty much a night person, so if it were totally up to me, your schedule would work just fine. Unfortunately, I do have to get up really early Monday through Friday, so Friday or Saturday nights would be the best for me."

"Okay. Then how about Friday night, I pick you up at 9:00? Where do you live?"

Clare hesitated out of habit – it felt odd to give out her address. But Paul already felt like he belonged in the not new date category, so she went ahead and gave it to him.

Suddenly there was noise coming from both the front and the back of the building, which meant the volunteers were there to serve, and the guests were ready to eat. Clare went to the front door, wanting to see Gus, while Paul went to greet the group.

Tonight, Tom was the first one in line. "Hey Clare - I got some good news!"

"What kind of good news Tom?" She loved seeing the smile on his face.

"I found a place to live. This senior citizen that needs help signed up to get a roommate, to help with chores and stuff, and I went to talk to him - I saw the sign on the door at the place I was going to register for assistance. Anyway - one of the clerks told me that maybe I could get in this program, where you trade chores for a room with an older person and I met the guy and we hit it off - and I'm moving in tomorrow!"

"Oh Tom - that is so great!"

"I know right? And listen - I'm going to keep coming around here sometimes, to help out, and you know - to talk to people. There's some good people here, ya know."

"I do know that." Clare said. It struck Clare that this was the first time any of the people she knew had made it off the street. Gus was at the back of the group waiting. After she greeted the other guests, she said, "Hi Gus. Would you mind coming to talk with me for a minute?"

He followed her toward the library. "Gus, I am glad you are doing so well. But I don't understand why you left so quickly, without even saying goodbye."

"I'm sorry if I hurt your feelings Clare. I was just afraid that if I told you I wanted to go, and you didn't think I was ready, that we'd have an argument. Don't get me wrong. I'm grateful that you let me stay at your apartment, and I'm grateful that you made sure I didn't have to go to some facility. But I needed to go home, and I was afraid you wouldn't let me do that." So - he did see the streets as home. That was what she'd thought he might say, but it still sounded odd to her ears.

"Look, Gus, I get that your life is your life. You don't have to answer to me at all. I just wish you would have trusted me to understand that."

"So, are you saying you think of us as equals Clare?" He questioned her, as if he didn't quite believe her.

"I do. Friends, actually. I guess it's not the same as it is with the people I typically have for friends. I can't call you on the phone and make plans. But I care about you, and I count on seeing you on Thursday nights. You matter to me. And I think I matter to you too. Isn't that a friendship?"

"I guess so. You do treat me like someone you care about. That's for sure. I really am grateful that you came to the hospital with me. That you sat with me when I was sick, that you helped me get out. But I don't see how I'm much of a friend to you. Doesn't really feel equal to me."

"Let me ask you something. If I had gotten sick, would you have run away, or would you have stayed and tried to help me?"

"Of course, I would have tried to help you."

"And I know you don't know that much about me, but do you realize you're one of the only people in Florida I can count on who will always say something nice to me, who would notice if I wasn't there?" As she made her case for friendship to Gus, Clare realized the truth of it herself.

"Okay, okay I guess what you're saying makes sense. And I get your point – I should have trusted you enough to tell you directly that I wanted to leave. I am sorry. And I'm sorry if I worried you. But as you can see, I'm totally fine, except at the moment I'm pretty hungry."  He smiled and nodded in the direction of the food line as if asking permission to end this conversation and get some dinner.

"Go, go. I'm sorry for holding you up. Whatever we're having, it smells delicious. You don't wanna miss it."

As Gus left, she looked around the room, and began to see the other regulars. Maria, Velma, their faces made her smile too. She'd never thought about these people as her friends before. But why not?  Why would someone have to have a home, to be a friend of hers? Maria and Velma, they were thoughtful, compassionate, never said a mean word to anybody. Maria would do anything for her kids, just like most of the girls Clare grew up with who were mothers now.

Clare felt this emotion welling up in her. All the time she'd been working here, thinking she was treating everybody as equal, she'd been discounting the guests. Not seeing them as real people that were part of her life. Watching Maria laughing with her kids, Clare felt like she'd been seeing the world in muted shades of grey. Now, all the colors were coming in. With fresh anticipation, she went to greet the new person at table five.

# Chapter 26

Clare got home before realizing that she'd made a date with Paul for Friday night - the same day Kate was coming in from the airport. What's more, like an idiot, she hadn't even gotten his number. So, she wouldn't be able to cancel without going over to Manna House – what a rude thing to do. She was particularly annoyed with herself for not even thinking about Kate, just because Paul asked her out. That wasn't the person she wanted to be – so enthralled with a guy she hardly knew that she forgot her own sister.

Clare opened her e-mail and saw that Kate was getting in at 5:00 – which was of course, the worst possible scenario – no time to get from work to Manna House, and then to the airport on time. She was just thinking she'd have to call over during the afternoon, and hope Paul picked up the main phone line, when the phone rang.

"Hey Clare – it's me. Did you get my e-mail?"

"Sure – I got it. No problem"

"Good! So, I'm really calling to find out how tonight went with the new guy."

"Paul. His name is Paul. Actually, it went pretty well."

"Fun flirting well, or asked you out well?"

"He asked me if I wanted to go out with him again."

"Great, when are you going?"

"I'm not sure."

"You're not sure?  How can you not be sure?"

She hesitated – no words came quickly to her mind.

"He asked you for while I'm in town, and you didn't want to say yes, right?"

"Kind of." Clare felt guilty that Kate was giving her more credit than she deserved.

"Stop it. I want you to go out with this guy while I'm in town. And I want him to pick you up, so I can see if he's worth your time and energy."

"But Kate, he asked me for Friday night. That's your first night."

"That's perfect. I'll be tired, ready to go to bed early. It's settled, you are definitely going."

Clare hesitated again – funny how it never felt right for her younger sister to tell her what to do. But this time, she decided Kate making the decision took away the guilt she would have felt, no matter what solution she came up with. So, she went with it.

"All right. I'll be there when you get off the plane. I really can't wait to see you."

"Me and my books will be there. Good thing Florida clothes don't take up much room in my suitcase. It would really add insult to injury if I had to pay for an extra bag just to lug my books."

After hanging up, Clare looked around the room, and realized that even though it was only Kate, and not her parents coming – she definitely needed to do some cleaning. Too late to put on loud music to make the time go faster, which left her cleaning with just her thoughts which were going about a hundred miles a minute.

She ran over the night at Manna House – and got stuck on those first few minutes, when she realized her role was going to change now that Paul was working there full-time. How could she be happy about Paul, and unhappy about the thing that brought him there?  It was a logical question – but this wasn't a logical topic for Clare. Somehow, Manna House had come into the gaps in her life, and filled her with – what?  A feeling of meaning maybe, or purpose?  Maybe the sense that she was doing what she was supposed to be doing?

Somewhere in her tired brain, Clare had the feeling that answers she hadn't even known she was looking for were beginning to come together.

# Chapter 27

Friday was a special day. Everybody had scheduled to work in the office, because it was the tenth anniversary of the firm. The partners brought in a catered lunch to celebrate. Teriyaki chicken and steamed rice, egg rolls and fried wontons, it was quite a feast. The ice cream sundae bar was a little over the top —the conference room carpet would never be the same. In a field where time literally is money, and parties mean no one is billing anybody – the gesture was really quite impressive.

Gary Grisham started in Clare's direction, which gave her a flashback to the office Christmas party. The guy was married, but he didn't let that fact get in the way of his trying to get to know the younger staff in every way possible. As far as Clare knew he'd never had any takers – his lines were older than he was. But nothing stopped this guy from trying.

"Clare, my love. You look better than ever. The sun of Florida certainly is agreeing with you."

"I do enjoy walking on the beach, particularly in the winter time."

"Perhaps you'd like a tour guide for one of those walks. I'm available to tell you the names of the shells and point out the plant life." At least he didn't ask if she wanted to come up and see his etchings.

"Thanks Gary – I do appreciate your offer – I'm sure you know a lot about the environment, but I have to say what I like to do is walk by myself and contemplate the waves."

He was already looking over her shoulder, to see who he might talk to next, so she let him off the hook easily, pretending to need to go to the ladies' room.

She saw Pete talking to the other seniors, and noticed he had a pleased tone to his voice. He seemed to know something no one else did, and he was enjoying the knowledge. Pete was climbing up the ladder these days. You could tell by the clients he got, that he was the one they were grooming for big things. The benefit for Clare was that she got to work on interesting clients and doing her best to make him look good wasn't a problem for her. He was a good guy – if anybody was going to have the inside track, at least it wasn't someone who tried to cut the corners with integrity. So far, most of the people she had gotten to know in the firm seemed to be on the up and up, but she knew enough to realize that there were always going to be people who would do whatever they needed to do to make a client happy – legal or not. Like Jack Anderson, the partner who told her to learn to make the numbers say what they needed to say.

After a few more minutes of eating and mingling, it was Jack Anderson who got up to speak. "Ladies and Gentlemen, we wanted to take this opportunity to thank you for the good work you've been doing this year, and in fact for the last ten years. We are grateful for your dedication and pleased to tell you that this has been the best year our firm has had yet. On your way out today, please pick up an envelope from the front desk, with a small token of our appreciation, for your dedicated service."

Spontaneous applause broke out – maybe for the gift, maybe just for the sense that in this impermanent world, this place had stayed open for ten years, and everybody here still had a job.

On the way to the airport, Clare opened the envelope and found a check for $1700. That was as much as she made in two weeks - better than a token in her book! And what a good time to get some extra cash. She'd be able to treat Kate, without her putting up a fight. The student loans Kate was going to end up with were high enough already without putting credit card debt for this trip into the mix.

Clare stood by security, happy to see that Kate's flight was supposed to be on time. She spotted her on the escalator, before Kate saw her. No one could miss her curly blonde hair - when they were younger she complained about it, said it made her look like a lion, but now it was one of her best features. As she got closer, Clare noticed Kate looked thinner than usual. The stress really must have been getting to her. Clare resolved to be her sister, not her mother, and not mention anything about the weight.

"Clare!  I'm so glad I came."

"Already?"

"Already. I slept on the way down – let go of all the stress – now I'm ready to just relax into mid-term studying on the beach."

"You want to take a spin by the beach on the way home? Paul isn't picking me up until after he finishes work at 9:00."

"Totally. But you're all dressed up."

"Oh – I always keep shorts and flip-flops in my trunk, should the chance to get out early present itself."

"Be prepared huh. I wouldn't have thought Mom's training sunk in that well."

"Well, the motivation for this one's pretty high."

"True."

"So – I've had a pretty interesting day. My bosses were celebrating the firms 10th anniversary, and they gave out bonuses. You got here at the right time! I can treat you to some good meals at the restaurants I've heard people talk about, but never had the guts to go in."

"Are you telling me the truth – or is this your way of getting me to let you treat?"

"Look at the envelope in my purse."

She found the envelope. "Wow – that's awesome. I won't let you spend it all on me – but I'll be glad to share in a little of the celebration."

They got to the beach, and Clare suddenly remembered the effect of the first of the February Break weeks. Traffic was a disaster. Clare pulled into the first parking spot she saw, knowing it would be quicker to walk than try to get closer.

"So, Kate – anything new happening in your life?"

"Oh – one or two things. I've been seeing a new guy – his name's Luke. He's fun, funny, and makes me take myself less seriously, which can be a temptation when you spend too much time with law students."

"So, he's not a law student?"

"No, he lives across the street from my apartment building. I met him walking his dog – he's got this chocolate lab that actually smiles when he sees me. Even if I didn't like him, I'd want to date him for his dog."

The sun was hot for this time in the evening. They got to the beach, and Clare quickly changed in the public bathroom, putting her dress clothes in her over-sized purse. She was tempted to lay it down as they walked, as most of the time Lido Beach felt safe. But Winter Breakers, and the check in her purse changed her mind.

"You really don't look very tan Clare. Does that mean you never get outside?"

"No, no – I just try to go out later in the day, like now. It didn't take me long living here to get sick of putting on sunscreen, and this is the best time of the night to watch the waves and see the sky."

"So, tell me the truth. Are you glad you made the move down here?"

"Definitely. Not that it's been easy. But I was just ready for a change, when I was getting out of school."

"Do you think you would have done this if you and Danny hadn't broken up?"

Clare thought about Kate's question for a minute, then said, "I don't really know. We used to talk about where we'd move after graduation in terms of where he could work - because we figured I had to follow him, since an accountant could work anywhere. But, yes, I guess wanting to get away from the memories and the questions did make me want to make a big change." She paused, thinking about Kate's question, and then decided it was time to tell her that she had seen Danny.

"Danny came here. He called me, and I met him after his set."

"I know. I'm glad you finally told me."

"What do you mean you know?  How would you know that?  I didn't tell anybody."

"I ran into Danny's sister at the mall, and she said - well she said he got a permanent job playing for a movie studio in L.A. and he's moved the wedding up - and she said he'd been to see you. What happened?"

"I'm surprised he told her. They must be closer than they used to be. Yes - he called, we met, we talked, he sounded like the same spoiled person I realized he was after we broke up, I left - and I cried what I hope were my last tears for him."

"Why did he call you? Was he trying to get back with you, or be friends with you?"

"Well - when I went - I thought it was to give us a chance to end things better than the first time. Not that I wanted to be friends, I just didn't love ending it the way we did. But as far as why <u>he</u> called - honestly - I think he was trying to figure out how to be a grown-up in his new relationship - and he wanted me to teach him how to do that. And truthfully, I didn't appreciate that request at all. In fact, I walked out on him. I guess the good news for him is that it sounds like he did figure it out - if he took a permanent job. And he's going through with the wedding."

Clare felt a little odd talking about Danny's wedding to somebody else – but it wasn't actually as bad as she would have thought it would be. Trying to lighten the tension, she said, "After all, he always said he wanted to get married. It was just me he didn't want to marry."

"Totally his loss!" Kate was having trouble holding back her emotions. They seemed to be a combination of anger and worry for how Clare was really doing.

"Spoken like a truly impartial person – who spent a lot of time letting me cry on her shoulder. Don't worry; I'm not going to fall apart again. He won't be getting any wedding presents from me, but it's not going to mess me up that he's moved on. I have too, in my own way."

As if on cue, two children's voices appeared behind them yelling "Clare, Clare!"

It was Maria's kids. They were running and jumping in the break of the waves right at the water's edge. Now, as they ran toward her, Clare noticed Maria rising from the beach.

The kids hugged Clare around the legs, and she laughed at how cold and wet they felt. "Hey guys. So good to see you!  I want you to meet my sister. Her name is Kate."

They shook her hand with their wet ones. Maria had reached them by then, and she wiped the sand off her hands to greet them as well.

"Maria, this is my sister Kate. She's on a break from school."

"Oh yes, I remember you said your sister was going to school to become a lawyer."

Kate was looking at her with questions in her eyes. She was clearly curious about this woman, who knew about her, that Clare had never mentioned. The kids began to look up the beach at something.

"Hey Clare, we're going to go dig a pool for the water to collect in. Wanna help?"

Maria laughed, "I think they are dressed a little too nicely for that."

"Remember when we did that when we were little, Kate?"

"Sure – you always made me do all the work – and then you wanted to jump in the pool first." The sly smile on Kate's face made Clare laugh out loud.

"Funny, that's not how I remember it."  She turned back to Maria.

"Enjoy your day. We're going to take a little walk, catch up a little, and get some color on this northerner's cheeks."

"We'll see you later Clare."  The kids waved, barely looking up from the engineering feat they were trying to accomplish.

When they'd gotten some distance away – Kate asked, "Who were those people?"

"Friends of mine."

"Where did you meet them?" Clare understood Kate's curiosity, but it felt somehow wrong to say Manna House. She felt like the stereotypes about homeless people might come up, and she didn't want to go there.

Finally, Clare said, "I met her through some of the volunteer work I've been doing."

"Oh – well she seems like a good Mom. Nice polite kids too."

After Kate said that, Clare realized that maybe this was a stereotype busting moment. "She is really nice, and her kids are terrific. Paola started school this fall, which must be hard to do, since they don't have a home to do homework in."

Kate looked at her quietly for a few minutes. Then she said, "They don't have a home?"

"No."

"So where do they sleep? They're just kids. They can't sleep on the street."

"Well, there are a few shelter programs in the area, but Maria has to be careful, because you can't take the kids to just any shelter. Some are pretty safe, with staff people around all the time. Others not so much. They spend most of their nights in the best one for families."

Kate got quiet again. Looking out at the ocean, she said, "A few minutes ago, I was feeling sorry for myself because I have to study over my break in Florida."

"I know what you mean. Don't feel guilty – that doesn't do anybody any good. Just get yourself out of law school and do something to make things better for people."

"Are you trying to tell me what kind of law to practice?" Kate smiled.

"No – do whatever kind of law you want. If you make lots of money – you can be one of those rich people who give their money away."

"Still sounds like you are trying to tell me what to do."

"Yeah well – I am your big sister – I should at least get a vote."

Kate gently pushed her toward the ocean – "I can't believe you're still playing the big sister card."

"You use what you got." Clare smiled.

Kate looked at her watch. "Do we need to be getting back? I don't want to make you late for Mr. Wonderful."

"Hey! I never called him that."

"Well, is he?"

"It remains to be seen. I feel like I kind of know him already, because I met him at Manna House – but that's not the same as trying to see if we fit as a couple."

"Do I get to meet him?"

"Will you make my life miserable if I don't introduce you?"

"Of course."

"Okay then – you can be there when he comes, and you can tell me what you think when I get home."

"That invitation I didn't need."

They cut up the beach to the sidewalk and headed toward Clare's car. She noticed people staring, in a way they didn't when Clare was alone. Kate had something – a look, a comfort in her own skin. She was beautiful, and you could tell she couldn't care less. When they were little, their Dad used to say that the only make-up anybody needed was loving life, and for the first time, Clare realized exactly what he meant.

# Chapter 28

Clare pulled out an outfit to put on. It was easy to choose – because she kept this particular outfit hanging in her closet, and only wore it on the rare occasion of a first date. The black one shouldered shirt, with the black pants; they made her feel confident. She added the sandals with heels that she would never wear any other time and decided to let her hair be long and free. At Manna House, she always wore it back, to make sure nothing ended up in the food. She added a silver necklace, with a large green stone, matching earrings and decided she was ready.

Kate smiled when she came into the living room. Since she'd been with Clare when she picked out the outfit, she recognized it. "That shirt really works for you. You look fantastic."

"Thanks for the totally unbiased review." Just then the doorbell rang, and Clare felt nervousness that she didn't remember feeling since she was about sixteen years old, and her parents met her first boyfriend.

Clare opened the door, to see Paul looking – well – tired. He smiled with his mouth, but his eyes looked really tired. She wondered what was going on – but didn't say anything right away. Instead, she just smiled and opened the door wide for him to come in and meet Kate.

"Paul – this is my sister Kate. She just got in tonight from up north. She's here to study."

"Let me guess. You thought studying on the beach would work better than at home."

"Exactly. Do you blame me?"

"Not a bit."

"Hey – how come you have a tan? Clare's always telling me people who live in Florida actually work during the sunny parts of the day – that it's only the tourists who get the suntans."

"She's right for most people. But I'm a second shift worker, from about noon to nine most of the time, so lately my mornings have a lot of beach time in them."

"Oh, that's right. Clare said you work at that place she volunteers."

Clare interjected, "Manna House. He's the new Director."

"Sounds impressive."

"Does it? Funny, to me it still sounds like a job nobody has actually defined." He was trying, but she noticed the look in his eyes again.

Kate picked up on the tone in his voice too. "Hm. You sound like somebody who needs to get out to dinner and relax. Why don't you guys get going? My books are calling me."

As they walked to the car, Clare decided to leave small talk behind.

"Hey – you look tired. Was it a hard night?"

"Well, I might look tired, but I'm really glad to be here with you."

So, he didn't want to talk about it. Or at least not yet.

He pulled the car out into the street, and then said, "Kate seems great."

"She's awesome. Fun to be around, I can talk to her about anything. She's the sister everybody else wishes they had."

"It must be hard to live so far from her then."

"I guess it would be, except I always expected to move away from home. When I was growing up, the economy in my hometown was always going through bad times. My friends' parents would lose their jobs, and sometimes they'd have to move away to get a new one. I remember thinking when I was pretty young that there might be other places that weren't so hard to keep a job in."

"Did it happen to your parents?"

"No. They were both long-time teachers, so pretty much the whole town would have had to move away for them to lose their jobs."

Looking around, Clare asked, "So, where are we going?" Truthfully, she was kind of surprised he hadn't asked for her opinion.

"Oh – I just started driving didn't I. Sorry. I was thinking maybe we could go to this restaurant on St. Armand's Circle. It calls itself Hemingway's – which I know doesn't mean he ate there – but still, I like the idea."

"Sounds good. It's on the list of places I haven't been yet, but always wanted to try." Which reminded her of her plan to visit some of that list this week with Kate, and her unexpected windfall. She told Paul about the party and the bonus.

"That's great! I like to hear stories where the money really does trickle down to us regular people."

He parked, and they started walking toward the restaurant. He was quiet again. Despite his efforts at small talk, she could see that whatever was wrong was right under the surface.

"Paul – how did it go at Manna House tonight?"

He looked around at her and saw the concern in her eyes lit up by the streetlights. "I really didn't want to tell you now, but I guess I stink at hiding things from you."

"Which, by the way, I consider a good trait."

He smiled, but only a little.

"Everything at Manna House was okay. It was what I heard that upset me. Apparently, Maria borrowed a car from a friend, and the rear taillight was out. The police stopped her, and she didn't have the right papers. They took her in, and the kids too."

"But I just saw them – not two hours ago, at the beach."

"Somebody said it happened on the way back from the beach. I guess she borrowed the friend's car to take the kids to the beach, and now she's in a lot of trouble."

"So – what do we do?"

"I don't know what to do. I don't know anything about this. She needs a lawyer, but there's no money for a lawyer."

"Do you think $1700 would get us an appointment with a lawyer that could help?"

"I guess that would be enough to get us in the door. Why $1700?"

"My bonus. I can't believe I got it today, and we need it tonight. How lucky is that."

Paul said, "You want to spend your bonus money on Maria?"

"Of course. My way of looking at things is that somebody bigger than me knew I was going to need that money to help somebody else. It's almost a miracle, when you think about it."

"What about your plans to take Kate out while she was here?"

"You're kidding, right. Kate won't mind waiting for her fancy dinners until she finishes law school and can treat me. But the next question is, who do we get?  Maria needs an immigration lawyer, I would guess - but I don't know anybody who specializes in that."

"I don't know anything about who we should get either. Maybe we could contact one of the non-profits who works with migrant workers and see who they use."

"Oh yeah, that's a great idea. My accounting firm does work with a group called Beth-El. They might be able to help us out."

"Do you think we could reach them tonight, see if they have anything we should do right now?"

"I think they probably do have some kind of an emergency hotline number. Let's check."

They were still standing on the street outside the restaurant, competing to see whose smart phone would come up with the contact info first. They hadn't had any food yet but working with Paul to try to figure this out – truthfully, it was already better than any first date she'd ever had.

# Chapter 29

They left a message at Beth-El's emergency line, then decided eating was still a good idea. Luckily, Hemingway's didn't have a wait. Clare didn't think she could have waited another hour for food. If she'd been smart, she probably would have had something to eat at 6:00. Now, she was starving.

As they walked up the steps that led to the restaurant and opened the door, Clare could smell some kind of a tropical smell. Coconut maybe – mixed with some other kind of fruit. Whatever it was, she wanted it. She looked around the restaurant, with it's sea green walls and the fishing nets serving as wall hangings - and felt like she was in a place where Hemingway could have written *Old Man and the Sea.*

The waitress approached them, saying "You're just in time. Our grill closes at 10:00, and we've got a fantastic grilled swordfish special tonight. It's in a coconut raspberry glaze if you're interested."

"I'm interested. How about you, Clare? Do you want that, or do you want to look at the menu?"

"No – I'll take that too – It smells amazing."

"And what about drinks? Would you like anything? The wine list is on the table. We have a chardonnay that would be nice with the swordfish."

"No thanks, not for me," Paul answered. She nodded her agreement.

The waitress left, and Paul said, "I'm not trying to be cheap about the wine. I just wanted to keep a clear head in case Beth-el calls back."

Paul went on, "I'm sorry that this date is turning into such a strange evening. I was really looking forward to just being with you, getting to know you better, outside of what we do together at Manna House."

"Well, look at it this way. Sometimes you get to know people best in the middle of a crisis."

"You do realize this is Maria's crisis – not yours or mine."

"I know – but still – Maria is my friend, and her kids feel like family, not just to me, but to all the Manna House regulars. This is my crisis, in the sense that it matters to people that matter to me."

Suddenly Paul's phone went off. He reached in his pocket, and grabbed it, and nervously hit the answer button. From his side of the conversation, she could tell it was some kind of answering service. He explained the emergency he was calling about, then hung up.

"The woman said they have a social worker on call. She's going to have him call me back."

"Well – I guess that's better than nothing."

"Yeah. I think this woman's point was that he could tell us what they do when they get people in this situation."

They both got quiet for a minute. It was hard to turn this back into any kind of normal evening at this point, but that seemed the only option while they waited for the next call.

"So, how was Gus tonight?" Clare asked, trying to fill what seemed like too long a space of quiet.

"He really seems fine, physically. He got very upset about Maria though. Kept telling me that he wanted to help. I don't know what he thought he could do, but he asked me several times to come find him if I thought of anything. He told me where to look for him, gave me a list of where he expected to be all weekend."

"You're kidding. That's totally not Gus."

They got quiet again, then Paul said, "Okay – so I said I wanted to get to know you outside of our Manna House connection. So, tell me something you do that has nothing to do with Manna House."

"Well, you already know I read."

"Right."

"And you already I know I'm an accountant."

"Right."

"And you already know I have a sister."

"Okay, I get the point that I do know some things about you. Tell me something - else - like maybe how you ended up living in Florida for example."

"Well - I came to Florida because there was a voice in my head that said a fresh start was what I needed - and I had all these good memories of vacations here - and here I am."

He looked intrigued - and like she hadn't come close to answering his question. So, she tried one more conversation ending statement. "I had a broken relationship right about graduation time - and I needed a fresh start. Okay?"

"Okay - I'm sorry, I wasn't really trying to pry."

"Yeah - you kind of were." She smiled.

"I really am sorry - I just wanted to understand how a Michigan girl ended up down here."

"Me and all the other retirees and snowbirds - the migration path is famous - it's just my timing that was a little different."

And Clare moved on to safer ground.

"Oh, here's something else. I'm a huge baseball fan," Clare said.

"Seriously."

"Yup. The Detroit Tigers. And since I've been here, I've started getting into the Rays. I watch on television and I love to go to games. My favorites are when the Tigers play the Rays, but I'll pretty much go to any game."

"With friends, or by yourself?"

"I've gone with groups of people from work a few times, and that's what made me decide that a game was something I could enjoy by myself. Particularly day games."

"Can I just point out that baseball is a really slow sport?"

"Not if you pay attention. Every at bat is a strategic battle between the pitcher and the batter."

"Come on. You have to admit it's a slow game."

"Spoken like a typical over-stressed, if I'm not busy every second I'm worthless American."

"Ouch!"

Clare laughed and asked, "What about you?  What don't I know about you?"

"I should have known that question was coming and had an answer ready. Let me think."

"What - Are you trying to come up with the perfect answer?  Just give me the first thing that pops into your head."

"I play the piano."

She felt her breath catch at that — but tried hard to make her voice even and normal. But seriously — did it have to be the piano?

"You play the piano. You play the piano like classical, or Broadway musicals?  Or you took piano lessons when you were a kid?"

"I play the piano pretty well."

"Okay – given that what I know about you so far is that you are a fairly humble guy, I'm guessing 'I play the piano pretty well' means you are amazing."

"Remember I told you I went up north to go to school?"

"Yes."

"Well, I got a minor in music. I would have majored in music, but everybody convinced me to make sure I had a practical degree."

"Why do people do that?"

"Because they want to make sure you can eat."

"Or maybe because they want to make sure they won't have to support you financially for the rest of their lives."

"Either way – for me it was good advice. Cuz the truth was I love music, but I want to do it when I want to do it, play what I want to play. I don't want to practice what somebody else picks out. That was okay when I was learning, but eventually I just didn't enjoy working on things that didn't move me anymore. I guess what that means is for me, playing the piano is something I love to do, not something I want to have to do."

"So, do you play now?"

"I have a piano in my apartment, and I play sometimes at my church, when the regular organist needs a sub. I play the piano, not the organ, but people seem okay with that."

"You have a church?  That's something else I didn't know."

"Uh huh. I went with my family growing up, youth group all of that stuff. Then I kind of drifted away. You know when I went back?"

"Well, I know the typical answer is when you had kids, but if you have kids that would break the bank on things you haven't told me."

"No, no kids. It was when there was a peace march in Tampa, and it started at one church and ended at another. I started thinking that I needed something in my life that would help me stand up for the things I believe in."

"That's funny. My sense would be that most of the churches around here would never get involved in a peace march."

"I know – but these two did."

His phone rang, and it took Clare a second to remember who would be calling, but Paul grabbed it right away.

She couldn't tell much about the conversation from listening to him. She got out a pen and a scrap of paper from her purse, in case he needed it, and at one point he grabbed it and started scribbling something down.

Their food came while he was still talking. Clare thanked the waitress quietly, and she smiled and nodded back. She sure had a sense of when to engage, and when not to interrupt. Impressive.

Paul hung up. "Well, that was helpful. Not particularly hopeful, but helpful."

"So, what did he say? I'm taking it that was the social worker."

"Yes. He said she's in big trouble. He said we need to get a lawyer immediately. He gave me some names that we can call first thing in the morning, and see who has time in their schedule, and would be willing to take the case. One question he had that I didn't know the answer to was where the kids were born."

"I think they were born here, in Florida. Maria's been here for a while, and the kids are four and five. Does that help?"

"Yes and no. It means they can't legally deport the kids, but that doesn't mean they won't deport Maria."

"But who would take care of the kids if they deport Maria?"

"I don't know. Foster care I guess."

"Could Maria choose to take them with her?"

"She could, but the social worker said some people don't if they have the sense that when they go home, it won't be safe for the kids, or that there won't be enough food."

The tactful waitress came by. She smiled at them, and said, "Boy, you two look worried. Whatever it is, you might want food in your stomachs to deal with it. Mange, Mange, before it gets cold."

They started to eat, and the taste sensation was intense enough to get Clare's attention. The swordfish was done just right, juicy and not too tough, but totally done. And the fruit sauce made her mouth happy.

"Wow." Paul said.

"This is incredible. Can we come back here, when we're not quite so distracted?" Clare surprised herself, being so bold as to assume they'd go out again.

"It does seem to be a place that deserves our full attention. I'm sorry about the way this night has turned out."

"Would you stop with that? Seriously – be quiet. I'm glad I was with you when I heard about Maria. I would hate to have been out with somebody who thought I shouldn't care about this woman - that people come and people go, or even worse that "illegal" people don't matter. This is exactly the way I want to be spending this night."

Paul looked at her with that look again. Like he didn't know what to make of her. She decided that she liked that look. She liked the idea of surprising this guy.

They left the restaurant, and started to walk to the car, and she felt his hand brush hers. Man, she hoped the little catch in her breath wasn't loud enough for him to hear. How embarrassing to get this excited over the slightest touch. And then she stopped feeling embarrassed, and just felt the touch of his fingers, and the arm close to her arm. They got to the car, and he moved away to open the door, and she actually felt sad.

Driving back to her apartment, Clare was kind of relieved that Kate was there. No stressing out about whether she should invite him in for coffee. She started to turn to say good night, and he was already getting out of his door. Seriously – was he going to walk her to her door? Had she ridden in a time machine without her knowledge?

Paul opened the door, and turned to her, "So – I know you said this wasn't such a bad night, but I really would like to have another chance at taking you to dinner. I'd like to hear all about your odd fascination with baseball, for example."

"Sure – but at some point, you're going to have to play the piano. I need to know if I'm having dinner with what could have been a famous pianist, who threw it all away."

"Dinner yes – dinner music – not so much. You'll have to know me for a long time before you have that experience."

"Unless I show up at your church on a Sunday when you're playing."

"FYI – there are lots of churches in Tampa. It could take you a long time to find mine." He laughed, and then his face became serious again.

"I'm going to call you tomorrow. I'll call the lawyers in the morning, and if anybody calls me back on a Saturday – that's our person. Sound like a plan to you?"

"Yes."

"Okay. Good night Clare."

"Thank you for the very nice evening." Geez she sounded like an etiquette school graduate, instead of the grown woman she wanted to be."

Clare thought he was just going to say, "You're welcome," and walk away. But instead he gave her a quick hug. And then he turned and walked back to his car.

"Good night Paul," She said quietly, with her hand on the doorknob. He heard her, turned, smiled and waved his hand, as he got in his car to drive away.

# Chapter 30

Kate surprised her by being asleep when she came in, which was probably a blessing. Clare didn't feel ready to do a post-mortem on the night. She just wanted to close her eyes and stay in the moment a little longer. She made a cup of herbal tea – something she hardly ever did – and sat in her favorite chair and just settled into the evening's memories. It was like she was making a mental picture album of the images from the restaurant, the car, the walk on the sidewalks of the Circle, and her own apartment's front porch. Becoming aware that she was sitting alone in a dark room with a smile on her face – it seemed like time to go to bed. But when she went to bed, the images changed. She started to see Maria and her kids. She started to wonder where they were, if they were all right. Were they together? Were they asleep right now? Finally, Clare found a way to some peaceful images in her brain, memories of walks on the beach that she'd stored as a happy place to go when she needed a ten-minute vacation from work or daily life. She went there, and let her tired body fall into sleep.

The loud noise woke her up very suddenly. Thinking she must have forgotten that it was Saturday and set it, she kept hitting the alarm clock snooze button, with no results, until Kate came into the room holding the phone.

"It's not the alarm sweetie. It's the phone. Apparently, somebody couldn't wait until a decent hour to call and say he wants to take you out again." Luckily, she had her hand over the receiver.

"Give me that." Clare said, lunging for the phone as if they were back in high school.

"Hello."

"Hi Clare. I hope I didn't wake you."

"Well, just a little. But it's fine."

"I'm sorry. It's just that I thought you'd want to know I got a call from an attorney already this morning. I tentatively set up a meeting with him at 1:00. Can you be there?"

"Definitely."

"Okay. I'll text you the address and meet you there about five minutes before."

"See you later."

Kate was watching her and raised her eyebrows at her part of the conversation. Clare realized that she knew nothing about how last night had been different than a typical date, and started to fill her in.

After a few minutes, Kate stopped her. "So, you're telling me that the woman we met on the beach yesterday is in deep trouble?"

"Yes. It's so hard to believe. She's been in this country for years and years. Now one busted taillight and she might have to go back to Mexico. I don't even know if she still has family there. I know she's not going to want to leave this country, because she's always hoped that her husband is still alive and will come back to her."

"So now you and Paul are going to get involved?"

"I hope so. We're going to meet with a lawyer that was recommended by some people who know about immigration issues."

"At the risk of interrupting a date, can I come?"

"It's not a date. Sure, you can come – why do you want to?"

"Because I'm in law school, reading about cases day in and day out. I want to see what it looks like when you actually bring a case to a lawyer, and they start working on it. Real law, that affects a real person I met yesterday. Yeah – I definitely want to see that. By the way, don't you have to pay this real lawyer at least a little real money?"

"About those fancy dinners I promised you…"

"I sense pizza and sandwiches in my future."

"Would you like some coffee? I've got that in the cupboard."

"Definitely."

Clare made the coffee, and since it was early – at least by Saturday morning standards, they went out onto the balcony to drink it in the not yet hot morning sun.

"So, was it a date at all last night?  Or was the whole night about Maria?"

"It was a date – just a different kind. And it was a good date."

"How good?"

"4 and a half star good. Great food, fun conversation – with the added benefit of seeing how compassionate he really is."

Kate looked unconvinced for some reason.

"What's the matter?" Clare asked.

"Well – I'm just wondering if this guy is so good that you won't ever make it past the friend stage. There's such a thing as too nice a guy you know."

"I don't agree with that at all. There's no such thing as too nice a guy! There is such a thing as a male friend – I'll give you that. But it's not because they are too nice. It's because the attraction isn't there."

"So, you are saying the attraction is there? How can you tell?"

Clare felt her face getting red. Since childhood – she'd had this embarrassing blushing issue when it comes to relationships. Clare had been hoping she'd outgrown it. But no.

Kate smiled. "Okay – I'll just take your word for it. Or I should say, I'll take the red color on your cheeks' word for it."

"Don't you have some studying to do?"

"Fine, I'll leave it alone. And yes, big sister, I've got my stuff all set-up on your dining room table."

"All right. Have to say, there are times when I envy you being in school, but Saturday mornings when I don't have to work – never one of those times. And this is the last one of those I'm going to have for a while. I think I'll walk over to Starbucks and pick up a paper."

A little bit of ambition hit her, and Clare decided to run instead of walk. Exercise hadn't been exactly getting its fair share of her attention lately. She felt like she was running on empty by the time she got to the coffee shop. Breathing hard, and totally sweaty, she hesitated to go in – except for the fact that there would be air conditioning on the other side of the door.

What she hadn't expected on the other side of the door was Gus.

Gus, sitting at a table with a man she knew! He was the counselor from the counseling center - she couldn't remember his name, but she knew it was him. The man was dressed for work, and Gus – well Gus was dressed the way he usually was, except he didn't have his sweater on.

Suddenly she flashed back to the moment in the hospital when Gus said his full name. August Andrews. That was it – that was the same name that had been on the counseling center check. What in the world was going on?

Gus's back was to Clare, and she backed away from where they were sitting to the other side of the store – where the line wound around to the order desk. She didn't know why she didn't want them to see her, but she knew that she didn't. It felt like it would be an intrusion. A huge intrusion into whatever was true of Gus' life that she didn't know. That he didn't want her to know. As curious as she was, Clare was surprised to find that her respect for Gus' privacy won out over her own need to know.

Still, as she tried to position herself behind other customers – Clare couldn't help trying to see the look on Gus's companion's face. Dr. Porter, wasn't that his name? Was he happy, worried, did he want to be sitting there with Gus? He was a little inscrutable, probably years of practice as a counselor. But then she saw Dr. Porter reach into his pocket and lay an envelope on the table. And Clare knew, she was sure, that there was a check in that envelope.

He got up then – and smiled at Gus. He didn't hug him, or shake his hand, but he did touch him on the shoulder as he said goodbye. She couldn't see Gus' face, couldn't gauge anything from his reaction. As Gus started to get up, Clare ducked behind a newsstand, until he was safely gone. Whatever was going on – she didn't want to find out this way. She wanted to know more about Gus when Gus wanted her to know more. Whenever that might be.

"Miss, miss – did you want some coffee?" The man behind the counter looked amused.

"Oh – yes. I'm sorry."

"No, I'm sorry. Looks like we made you wait in line so long, you forgot you came here for coffee." He dug in his pocket and pulled out two tickets. "Here – the next two coffees are on us."

Clare thanked him, took the coupons – ordered her latte, and sat down to rest her feet and her imagination. She saw the New York Times lying next to the upholstered chair and started reading the op-ed page. It was an article about homelessness – and suddenly – she didn't want to think about that topic anymore. Her head was beginning to hurt with all the thoughts that were going around in there. She picked up the sports page – and read about the Tigers coming to Lakeland for spring training. Baseball news - that was the diversion she was looking for.

# Chapter 31

Clare got ready for the appointment, wondering what Paul would think about bringing Kate along. Personally, she liked the idea. Kate needed to see what real law looked like. Clare totally got that. Staying in the books all the time could make you pretty crazy. And from her perspective, she didn't like the idea of having a combination lawyer's visit/date.

Kate came in, saying, "Hey can I borrow something to wear. I don't think shorts and a tank top would be appropriate for a lawyer's office."

"Sure – no problem." Going through her clothes, Clare realized that way too many of them were accountant gray. It seemed to be an unwritten rule of her office – one that had apparently seeped into her closet without her knowledge. There was one navy above the knee skirt she thought Kate might look good in – and a blouse that had some kind of purple flowers on it. For herself, she chose a dress that she'd picked up in her last year of school, during interview season. It was beige, with a belt, and it had the look of quiet confidence that she loved. She used to tie a scarf around it in Michigan, but here – she thought her big brass pendant necklace would work better.

Kate and Clare stood together at the mirror, and she could see the resemblance that wasn't always so noticeable. A casual observer might be thrown off by the difference in their hair colors and the fact that Kate's was curly and huge, and Clare's was rather straight. Clearly though, they were related when you looked at the big blue eyes, the identical noses and the shape of their mouths. They even smiled alike.

"I know I'm being selfish, asking to come along, but I gotta tell you, I'm really excited."

"I'm glad you're coming. Really. And I'm sure Paul will understand too."

Noticing that the office was in a part of town she wasn't familiar with, Kate and Clare left early to get to the lawyer's office on time, in case they got lost – and made it so early as to be a little embarrassing. Their Dad always taught them not to be late - but figuring out what to do when you arrive this early was a problem Clare hadn't quite solved. They parked far away, so that they could take up the time with a walk to the office.

Paul pulled up just as they were arriving at the door – and found a place right in front.

Kate spoke as soon as he got out of the car. "I begged Clare to bring me along. Hope that's okay. I just really wanted to see law happening outside my books. And who knows, maybe immigration law will turn out to be my thing."

Paul smiled at her, "Oh its fine. I don't think the lawyer will mind having another person in the room."

Actually, the lawyer's office was quite small. There were only two chairs, and no room to pull in a third, so Kate stood next to a file cabinet as they began the meeting. Clearly, immigration law didn't pay well, at least not the way this lawyer practiced it.

The lawyer shook each of their hands as they came in the room, then said, "I'm Stan Myers. I've been practicing immigration law for twenty years. I work with the Beth-El folks a lot and I'm here to get the best outcome for your friend I can. First things first, I want you to know the facility your friend's been taken to is decent."

"What about her children?"

"They are in the same facility. She's able to see them, although at night they are separated."

He went on, "We've got several things going for us on this one. Her children were born here. That means they are citizens. Although there are horror stories about kids being left behind while their parents are deported, most people realize that's not the best thing. So, if we can find any reason for the courts not to separate a family, most of the judges I've appeared before will jump on that reason." He stopped talking for a moment to let them catch up with that he was saying.

Paul said, "You said Maria had a couple of things going for her?"

"Right. The other thing she has is you people. Having people who know her, who will speak for her that can make a big difference. How do you know her and how long have you known her?"

"I've only known her for a few weeks, but Clare's known her for longer."

"I've known Maria and the kids for a few months now. They really are great people."

"How did you meet her?"

"Well – I'm a volunteer at Manna House. It's a program that provides food for homeless people."

"So, you think she's been homeless for how long?"

"A year, maybe a little longer. Since her husband disappeared."

"Yeah – that's the part that we don't have going for us. Homeless, not knowing what happened to her husband means people could try to say all kinds of things about their family. And – it could also be that the story isn't good. Maybe he's a drug currier. Maybe he was – killed while doing something illegal. You see what I'm saying."

Paul said, "Or maybe he left his family because the guilt of not providing for them got to him, and he couldn't stand putting his kids to bed hungry every night." Clare could tell Paul was thinking about the woman he'd met up in Brandon. That experience had definitely left its mark on him.

"It's possible. Anything is possible. Which is why I'd like to use some of the money you give me as a retainer to get a private detective. I'm assuming nobodies' ever done that in this case."

"No. Maria's tried to look herself, but nothing official," Clare said. She pulled out the check for his retainer, and he agreed that $1700 was enough to proceed with the case in the way he'd been describing.

They could hear people in the small lobby getting restless, and the attorney was rising to let them leave, but Clare had another question.

"Can we visit Maria? Where is she?"

"You can put in to visit her. She's in the detention center in Moore Haven. It's called Glades. They have visiting hours, and they explain their procedure on-line. Follow every step they say, because if you don't you aren't getting in."

"Okay – thanks."

He waved to dismiss them, as he put Maria's file to the side, already looking at what was coming next. Clare liked his intensity – he seemed like he knew his work, and she got the sense that he would do his best to help Maria.

In the lobby there were a variety of people, different in ages, different in the languages they were speaking to each other. But they had one thing in common. A look in the eyes that was some combination of fear, and desperate hope that the man they were about to see might actually be the one that could make the fear go away.

# Chapter 32

"So – I don't have to be at work until later. Anybody interested in some ice cream?  We have a great place on the circle, Kate."

"Seriously Paul – do you ever eat at home?"  Turning to Kate, Clare said, "He's been in town like a day and a half, and he knows about things it took me months to find."

"You're not seriously comparing ice cream from the grocery store to ice cream from an ice cream shop, are you?"

"Of course not. Any true ice cream lover knows that the place on the circle is beyond compare."

Kate smiled - "Well now I have to go – just to see if it's as good as you two are saying."

Kate and Clare got in her car – and followed Paul to the circle. Kate tried to get Clare to drop her off, and make it into a date, but Clare told her that would make her look a little desperate, since he invited both of them. Plus, truthfully, she wanted Kate to spend a little time with Paul, to see what her radar told her about him.

They went in, and ordered waffle cones covered in chocolate, filled with homemade ice cream that was insanely rich, and incredibly creamy. There was a small table open, and they decided to sit for a minute, so their ice cream wouldn't melt too fast in the sun.

"So, Kate – how was that meeting from the 'I want to be a lawyer' perspective?"

"Fascinating. I liked the way he was already anticipating the things that could make trouble for Maria and trying to be the most prepared person in the room when he gets a chance to go to court. I have to say, we don't discuss the role of private detectives much in school. We're more into the case law, and how decisions get made. This helped me see what goes into the preparation of a case. I've heard the advice never ask a question you don't already know the answer to – I guess I just haven't thought much about how it is that I could know the answers."

"Sounds like law school is very theory focused, and for the practical part, you're supposed to figure that out for yourself?" Clare asked.

"Well at least at this point. I'm still pretty early in my program, remember."

Clare smiled at her, "Still - that sounds a lot like when I finished school, and started working for an accounting firm, and thought about getting a C.P.A. to do my taxes. Degree in accounting, yes – practical ability, not so much."

With the ice cream reduced to a manageable size, they went outside to walk around the circle, and see in the windows of the shops that were beyond all three of their budgets.

"Okay – here's a question for you. You have $10,000 and you have to spend it in one of these stores. Which one, and what would you buy?" Kate could make a game out of anything.

"Can I buy gift cards?" Paul asked.

"I see where you're going with that. You're thinking you can put the money away toward your Christmas present and birthday gifts for the next five years. Very tricky. No way - $10,000 – today. That's the question."

"All right – I'll go first" Clare said. "I'd buy the purple jewelry in that window for me, and turquoise for you and the pearls for Mom. Dad would be out of luck I guess. I can't see him wearing cufflinks even if they are diamond studs."

Paul looked around. "$10,000. That would buy me a lot of clothes in that Bahama store over there, which I'm pretty short on. I could have a wardrobe for life."

"As long as you don't gain any weight." Kate said.

"Excuse me – I resent the implication that I'm on the road to the middle-aged spread."

"Well…if you keep eating that ice cream…"

Paul laughed, and Clare felt the peace that comes when you know people you like are getting along. Kate was not always a fan of people Clare went out with – too stuffy, she'd say. Or too egotistical. Or too boring. With Danny - the egotistical label had never really gone away in Kate's opinion. In fact, come to think of it, Kate was never a fan of anybody Clare went out with.

"What about you Kate?  You can't get out of answering the question, just because you asked it."  Clare reminded her.

"See that store over there. The really cool gift shop with the African motif. I want that vase and the colorful cloth it's sitting on. It's amazing!  I bet it would cost $10,000, and it would still fit in my suitcase to take home. It would go in my dorm room, and in the Manhattan office I'll have some day."

"New York. Really?  Is that a joke, or do you really think you want to stay back east when you finish school?" Clare asked.

"Well, I don't need to move down South, since I can always visit you when I want the sun. And truthfully, I like the pace of the Northeast. I like feeling like every day matters, maybe even every minute matters." .

"Funny, I've never heard anybody say that. I always hear complaints from my friends who stayed up north after they finished school."  Paul looked surprised, and a little intrigued.

"Yeah – well maybe in a few years I will feel that way. But I don't think so. I think it's how I'm wired."

"I can see that," Clare agreed. "As someone who has known you forever, I can see you liking all the stimulation that would probably drive me nuts. And I can see you wanting every second of your life to count."  What she didn't say out loud was that she had a feeling this enjoyment of the fast-paced life was Kate's way of trying to make her life matter. Seeing life as a gift not to be wasted - maybe that was Kate's way of living out the faith they grew up with?  She thought she'd ask her later, but then…

"So, Kate do you go to church?" Paul must have heard what Kate said the same way she did, but she couldn't believe he just laid that out there. It wasn't something people usually did, in her life anyway.

Kate looked a little surprised, but she answered him, "I did growing up of course, like Clare. And I guess it affected me, because I tend to want to be on the side of people who need help, who don't have money or power, instead of the corporations, or the mega rich folks that need attorneys. The Manhattan office I was joking about wouldn't be a window office on 5th Avenue. I'm thinking more a storefront in an area where they need legal aid. But to answer your question – no – as of now I don't go to church. I could give you lots of excuses about the busy-ness of law school, but I won't. It's just not where I am in my life right now."

See that was the thing about Kate. Never afraid to talk about anything. She wasn't shy – she didn't mind living a public life

– where the inside and the outside were exactly the same. Clare couldn't do that. Sure – she would have answered a question like that from Paul if he asked her – but if some guy she didn't know asked her, she would have found a way to change the subject. She would have thought 'It's none of his business. I don't want to talk to him about this.' What did that say about her? Why was she so much more guarded than Kate? They grew up in the same house, went to the same schools. But somehow, Clare came out worried about how people would respond to her, careful with every word, and Kate came out not thinking about that at all, at least as far as she could tell.

"Clare – are you in there?" Kate was laughing at her. "Just so you know Paul – Clare has a whole other galaxy going on inside her head. And apparently, it's a wonderful place to be, because she goes there pretty often."

"I know just what you mean. My family always said they could tell when I went on a trip to Planet Paul. Pretty inconvenient when it happens in the middle of class though." He looked at her with this knowing, affectionate look, and she felt her cheeks turn red.

Kate looked back and forth between them for a minute. "Which reminds me, you two might not have anything on your agenda this afternoon, but I've got some book learning to do. Thanks for the real-world experience today. Clare, want to give me your keys? I could find my way back, and then maybe Paul could drop you off later, when he goes in to work."

Clare didn't have time to feel embarrassed by Kate's assumption that Paul wanted to spend more time with her. Kate took the keys out of Clare's purse pocket – and was gone as soon as Paul finished saying he'd be glad to drop her off.

"So – where to now?" Paul asked.

"Well – a walk on the beach might be nice. We're a bit overdressed, but it's not too hot today."

"I like it. Let's go."

They decided to leave the car parked where it was and turned toward Lido Beach. When they got there, they left their shoes by the boardwalk and started toward the ocean shoreline. The place was more packed than usual. The kids were making castles, trying to make pools of water by the edge of the ocean. One little girl was writing something in the sand with her finger, and her brother was drawing a picture. Clare stopped to see the picture, and Paul kept going for a minute, before he recognized she'd stopped.

"It's beautiful. It's a starfish, right?"

"Yes," the boy said, with a big smile because she'd been able to identify it.

"Don't talk to strangers Jason," his sister said, looking at her in suspicion. And the boy's joy suddenly evaporated, with fear quickly taking its place.

"Oh – I'm sorry," Clare said, looking around for parents to reassure, but not seeing any right there, she just turned back to walking with Paul.

"You okay?" Paul asked.

"Yeah – I'm okay. I'm just sad."

"I know what you mean. Hard to imagine a future where people know how to get along and take care of each other, when parents teach their kids to be afraid of everybody on sight."

"On the other hand – what would I teach my kids if I had any? I get it. I just hate it."

"But would you really teach your kids to be afraid of everybody?  Isn't there any other option?"

"Well, it's pretty hard to teach little kids which strangers are okay, and which ones they should be afraid of. So which side do you err on?"

"I guess I hope I can figure out how to be on the side of love, instead of the side of fear."

"Isn't that easy to say, when you don't have any kids you're responsible for."

"That's the thing though. Parents aren't just responsible for keeping their kids alive. They are supposed to help them grow into good people, caring people, compassionate people. You work with homeless people, you know how people look at them, treat them when they meet them on the street. No respect, or love, or sense that they are even people. They are just objects – to be feared and avoided."

"But the thing is, my parents taught me not to talk to strangers, and like you said, I work with homeless people. There's a way to teach your kids personal safety, and compassion."  Clare stopped - realizing that their voices had been getting louder and louder. She turned toward the ocean, looking at the huge waves for a minute. "There's lots of ways to teach your kids how to be loving people, without putting them in danger."

Paul smiled, but it wasn't a happy smile. "I'd like to agree with you, but the way I see it, life is dangerous. The paths are filled with choices, and if you teach your kids too much about fear, then the choices they make will be all about avoiding the things they are afraid of."

"I still think you have to teach your kids what you just said – that life is dangerous. But somehow – the lessons about love need to be strong enough to fight back the fear."

"I guess you're right that I can't just tell my kids to love without explaining the flip side – that loving can be dangerous." He paused. "Why do I feel like people with kids would be laughing at all this theoretical conversation, when they have to live life day-by-day. One of my friends said he always feels like he's working without a net. He told me he and his wife had been joking about saving for therapy instead of college, given the mess they figured they were making out of the whole parenting thing."

It occurred to Clare that she'd never had a discussion like this before. Even with Danny – the furthest they'd ever gotten was imagining how many kids they would have. Had she grown up this much – or was this guy just deeper than anyone she'd ever gone out with?

Paul looked at his watch. "We better head back to the car. It's almost time for me to get ready for work."

"Are you fully staffed for tonight?"

"We are. We've got a group from Church of the Palms, and the records say they always bring a bunch, so we should be good."

While they were talking, Paul seemed to move closer, and she felt his fingers brush her hand. Instinctively, she leaned in instead of away, and this time he took her hand. Truthfully, this was Clare's favorite part of dating – the first time holding hands. It's like there's all this promise of closeness, just beginning. A first kiss - that can be great. Handholding, it's like a commitment that more will follow – and with this guy – she definitely was deciding she wanted more to follow.

# Chapter 33

When she got home, Kate was hard at work on the balcony. Clare cut up some veggies, poured out some dip, and took them out to give her a break. "Hey Turkey!  Pretty embarrassing move you pulled there, leaving Paul no choice but to spend more time alone with me."

"Oh yeah. You really hated it."

"Well – I didn't say I hated it. I just said it was embarrassing."

"So – how did it go?"

"Good I think. We argued over something that happened on the beach – and it was actually good. I felt like we heard each other, and we could disagree without it being a catastrophe. I gotta say – that's not an experience I've had very often."

"Yeah – me either. For some guys, it's like if the woman is smart enough to argue well with him, he doesn't want the competition."

"Must make law school a tough place to date."

"There all anybody wants to do is argue. And everybody is always going for the win – take no prisoners. I haven't totally ruled dating law students out, but you notice I'm dating my neighbor."

"With the awesome dog."

"Exactly."

"So, what are you working on?"

"Reviewing cases for my contracts class. Although what I feel like doing is reading immigration law."

"I know – I was thinking I'd go in and look up the rules about visitation at that detention center where Maria is. I wonder if she feels like no one knows where she is, like the way it was with her husband."

"Did you say you knew him?"

"No. He was gone long before I came around Manna House. Knowing Maria, it's hard to believe anything bad about who he was could come out. Still, I'm glad the attorney's thinking ahead. And who knows, maybe his private investigator will figure out something that would help Maria know what happened to Roberto."

Looking online, Clare located the detention center, and read about visitation. The center was a couple of hours away. The photos online didn't look too terrible, more like an old elementary school than the jail she'd been picturing. But it still made her feel sick to her stomach, imagining Maria and the kids there. She turned off the screen, not wanting to see it anymore.

Then she picked up a book she'd been reading, and rejoined Kate on the balcony. Kate was totally absorbed in her work, and Clare soon lost herself in the book, until the sun started to get lower in the sky, and they both noticed they were hungry.

"So – I gave away our fancy eating budget – and there's not much in the refrigerator. Want to find a place we can get a slice of pizza? Or if you want to keep working, I can order in."

"If you don't mind – ordering in would be awesome. I promise to talk to you over the food – but I'm really into this, and I don't want to lose my momentum."

"You got it." Truthfully, ordering in sounded good to Clare too. She felt peaceful and comfortable hanging out in her apartment with Kate, and she'd been out enough in the last few days to appreciate relaxing. She ordered pizza without interrupting Kate any further – assuming that the order they'd grown up with hadn't changed for either of them. If she was wrong, at least they'd have a nostalgic meal.

When the food got there, and they sat down to eat, Kate said, "So – I'm surprised at you. You've hardly been obsessing at all over Paul. Is that a good sign or a bad sign?"

"Partly, it's a respect for your studying, and partly, I'm finally trying to take your advice not to over think this one."

"And you're listening to me because..."

"Because I don't want to mess this up. I like Paul enough to try something new, and just wait to see where it's going, instead of asking myself, and ultimately him the question that tends to freak people out."

"Yeah, I've only known one person who made, 'where do you think this relationship is going' work for her."

They both said at the same time. "Mom!"

Laughing together, Kate and Clare retold the story to each other. In their parent's story there was this moment, when their

Dad had gotten a job out of state. Their Mom had asked him 'the question' and the next day Dad showed up with a ring and a proposal, as the answer she'd been waiting to hear.

Changing the subject, Kate said, "Hey, I saw that card on the bulletin board – have you been going to church?  I don't think I heard that news from Mom and Dad."

"Yes, I've tried it a few times. It's really different."

"What was so different?"

"Candles, quiet – I don't know – kind of a less is more theme I guess. Very counter cultural. You want to go?"

"Actually, what I'd really like to do is go see Manna House. I want to see this place that seems to be taking up a lot of your mental energy these days."

"Okay sure. We could do that. "

Clare shooed Kate back to her books after dinner. But she couldn't stop thinking about what Kate had said. It was true - her head and her heart were living more and more at Manna House. Those people, their lives, they mattered to Clare. It wasn't that her job didn't matter to her when she was at work - but when she walked out those doors - it was Manna House and its' people - from Gus to Maria to Velma and now Tom and of course Paul - it was those people who were on her mind.

# Chapter 34

Sunday night they went over to Manna House at dinnertime. Clare showed Kate around, introducing her to a few folks, looked for Paul to say Hi. Clare didn't expect him to be able to stop and talk, and she was right – Sunday dinner was pretty much a zoo, because lots of people missed dinner on Saturday.

"We don't want to bother you – I just wanted Kate to see the place." Paul had a look on his face she couldn't quite read.

"So – you want to get a really first-hand view?" Paul asked Kate.

"What did you have in mind?"

"We had two small church groups scheduled to work today, and one of them didn't show up. I could really use some more hands. Could you spare an hour?"

Clare hesitated, not sure if Kate could spare another hour from her books – but Kate quickly said, "Of course."

"Thanks. Right over here. I just need you to bring the bowls of seconds to the tables. Otherwise, people start coming up looking for more, and we get a traffic jam of hungry people at the kitchen door."

They started circulating. Actually – Kate was glued to Clare's elbow. She was looking at the bowls – but not really the people. Hard to believe this was a setting that intimidated her confident sister – but the evidence was pretty unmistakable. Of course - the first night Clare had worked at Manna House had not been a sterling moment for her either.

They filled up a bowl of corn, then some mashed potatoes. The hot open-faced turkey sandwiches were a big hit. Whoever put this meal together had done an awesome job making the kind of comfort food that people loved. Clare saw Gus, and was taking Kate over to meet him, when a huge crash stopped her cold.

A crowd gathered near the entrance to the room. Paul was already making his way there with the volunteer manager. Instinctively moving toward the noise, Clare heard Paul ask what happened.

"It's Velma. She passed out!" somebody screamed.

"Okay, everybody back up, and let's give her some air." Paul said.

The crowd moved away, to reveal Velma on the floor. She was still out.

Paul kneeled down beside her. "Velma. Velma do you hear me?" She was beginning to stir a little, but her eyes were still closed. "Velma – can you open your eyes? Does anything hurt?"

Velma nodded no, but her eyes were still closed.

The crowd was still staring, so Paul looked around and said. "Hey everybody, let's give her some space. Go ahead and eat. She's okay."

Some of the people moved back to their tables, but Gus and a few of the others who knew Velma well stayed put, waiting to see what she would need.

Velma coughed, and stirred a little more, and then finally opened her eyes.

"I'm okay." She said.

"Are you?" Paul asked. "You didn't hurt anything when you fell?"

"No – everything's okay."

"Any idea why you fainted?"

"Last time it happened, the doctors said I was anemic." Clare saw a look of understanding come into Paul's eyes. She wondered what he was thinking.

"So – we need to get some food into you? Is that the answer at the moment? Or should we get to the hospital?"

"Oh no I just need some of whatever that good smell is, and I'll be feeling fine in no time." Velma was maybe fifty years old, and one of the things Clare'd noticed about her was that she had the most positive attitude she could imagine anyone having, given the lifestyle she was living.

Gus came over and took her elbow to guide her toward a table. He looked at her with all sorts of kindness and concern.

Turning to Paul after the others moved away, Clare asked "Don't you think we should call an ambulance or something?"

"I don't think Velma wants that. And if she doesn't want it – I don't think she's in an emergency situation that calls for us to override her choice."

"Okay – I hear you. I get it that we need to give people as many areas of control as possible about their lives. But health issues?"

Paul looked directly into her eyes. "It's a health issue Clare. But it's not the one you think it is. It's one that requires the person involved to decide it's time to do something about recovering from their disease."

Clare heard what he was saying between the lines and wanted to argue with him. She knew Velma better than he did, and she'd never seen her drunk.

Clare turned to look at her again. On the other hand – maybe Velma was living from shelter to shelter and meal to meal for that very reason. Paul must have had a reason for saying what he said. What did she really know?

Clare suddenly remembered Kate at her elbow. She'd been quiet this whole time. It bothered Clare that this probably reinforced whatever thoughts had been making her fearful before Velma fell. On the other hand, people's stories are their stories. Kate would just have to deal with it.

They went back to serving, and when Clare got a chance she went over to Gus and Velma. Velma was laughing at something Gus was saying. Whatever anyone else saw at that table, Clare saw people who were there for each other, no matter what.

# Chapter 35

Work was starting to gear up, but Pete let her come in early and eat at her desk, so she could leave early enough to at least spend a little time with Kate in the evening. She didn't hear from Paul, which when she was feeling good about herself meant he was giving her space to be with her sister, and when she was in a bad mood meant he was never going to call again.

She wondered a lot about Maria and the kids and kept trying to figure out how to get time off to visit the detention center. Kate didn't say much about their time at Manna House, until the last night of her visit. They were at dinner on the circle, watching the people walk by the window, when Kate said, "So you really like volunteering at Manna House don't you?"

"Yes – but you didn't, and you don't see why I do. That's what you're trying to say right?"

"Well actually that was what I was trying to not say, but I guess I didn't succeed. I really don't get it Clare. I mean – I get helping people. I even get caring about somebody like Maria and her kids. But those people that you said you've known the whole time – that Gus and that Velma for example. How is it that you connect with people like them?"

Clare didn't like that Kate had said people like them. She didn't like it at all. But she decided not to react to the terminology, and just tried to answer the question.

"Kate, I gotta say, once you get to know people, we're all pretty similar underneath. The thing that happened with Velma, that's not a typical night, she's usually a pretty easy person to be around, but if she's a drinker, and if she told us her story, we'd probably understand why. And Gus, I know him pretty well, and he's just a really awesome person. I don't know his story either. And I've often wondered what he's doing on the street – but whatever it is the streets and the shelters haven't taken an amazing amount of human kindness out of him. I wonder if I'd do as well, if I was alone in the world, with no job, and no sense of how the future would be any more than a one day at a time struggle to survive."

"I guess. But you wouldn't be in that situation. You wouldn't let that happen, and if somehow your life turned into a mess, our family wouldn't let that happen."

"I used to think that too. I really did. But you'd be amazed how fast things can go badly in somebody's life. Like there's a guy. His name is Tom; you didn't meet him. He had a decent job, until he got in a car accident. He had so many injuries that he maxed out his insurance. Head injuries were part of it, so he couldn't go back to his old job. His parents were living in a retirement community, where no one under 55 could live, no matter what. They tried to get an exemption for him, but they couldn't. And they didn't have any extra money to help. So, he ended up moving into a shelter, trying to hold onto a minimum wage job and save up money for a one-room apartment. He could have been you and me."

"Is he still on the street?"

It was a good thing that Kate had gotten caught up enough in the story to want to know what had happened to Tom. It gave Clare hope, because she knew from experience that usually the best way to get over pre-conceptions – was one person at a time.

"No. He got into a program where you get a free room in a senior citizen's house, and for that you do their yard work, chores, and just make them feel less lonely. It's kind of a cool program. So, somebody like Tom, who can keep a job, can save up money. That way, if the senior citizen decides they don't want to stay in their home anymore, Tom has enough saved to make finding housing possible."

"Okay seriously Clare – do you put half as much energy into your job as you do learning all this stuff?"

"What are you trying to say?"

"I'm trying to say do you love the job you get paid for this much?"

"Hm. Do I love my job?  I don't know – it's a good question. I don't not love my job."

"Oh well that's a wonderful endorsement." Kate laughed at her double negative.

"Shush – I'll have to think about it, okay?"

"Okay – it's not a test you have to pass."

"Unlike your current life, is that what you're thinking?"

"I do feel like it's strange that you're out here with a real life and I'm still so far from that. School feels like it will go on forever, and then when I'm done, there's the Bar exam that I have to pass to actually get a job that will help me pay the ridiculous amount of student loans I'm going to have." Kate's expression matched the tone of her voice perfectly.

"Come on Kate. You know better than that. The time will go really fast, and when it's done, you'll be doing something you've wanted to do for your whole life. I don't think you'll have any trouble answering questions about whether you love your job."

"You know what did help? Seeing that guy, that lawyer you guys got to look into Maria's situation. Maybe that's what I need. Hands-on stuff. But no one will hire me now, and the school's not likely to have an internship for me – I'm not one of the law review type students."

"Well, if that's true, why don't you create your own?"

"What?"

"Find an attorney who needs volunteer help. Do filing, answer phones, greet clients. I bet there are plenty of legal aid people who could use a volunteer, and they'd probably be pretty flexible about the hours you worked, since they wouldn't be paying for them."

"You know what you just said would sound crazy to the people I hang out with on a daily basis."

"What do you mean?"

"Work for free?"

"Yeah – you know Kathryn if you're going to start now listening to those people, you're going to be doing things you don't care about for the rest of your life."

"I didn't say I would listen to them – that was just an observation. And don't call me Kathryn. You only call me that when you're disappointed in me, and it ticks me off." Her face was red.

"I'm not disappointed in you." Clare protested, realizing she'd pushed Kate too hard, given the week of studying she'd just put in, and the week of exams coming up.

"Yeah - I think you are." Kate was angry, but more than that she was hurt.

"Okay - I guess it's hard for me when you seem like you're buying into what other people think." Suddenly Clare shook her head. "Which is pretty funny when you think of it, because you've always been the one telling me not to worry so much about what other people think."

Kate smiled a little at that. "Yeah, when did we switch roles?"

"We didn't really - I know you'll end up doing what you think is right, no matter what those other law students think. You couldn't do life any other way."

"This is true." Now Kate was fully smiling.

Right at that moment the waitress showed up with a dessert menu that included chocolate, chocolate and more chocolate. They split a hot fudge brownie and enjoyed every bit.

As they drove back home, Clare said, "Kate – I'm not disappointed in you. I could never be disappointed in you. I'm sorry if I hurt your feelings."

"You didn't really. You just bugged me because you made me think about options to solve my problems instead of just agreeing with me that life isn't the way it's supposed to be. Do you know how annoying that is?"

"Totally – you're telling me I turned into Mom and Dad?"

"Yeah – so watch it, okay?"

"I promise. From now on, I'll ask permission before I give you advice."

"Okay, that's never going to work. Just be you, and we'll be fine."

They went back to the apartment, got her stuff, and were halfway to the airport before Kate started her part of the advising. "So, what do you think your next move is with Paul?"

"Wait for him to call me, to make sure he really wants to call me."

"Okay, I would think that was a bad plan no matter what, but it won't even work for you. You've got Manna House dinner tomorrow night. Remember?"

"Which gives him an easy way to ask me out if he wants to do that. So, if he doesn't, I'm sure not going to ask him."

"What is this, the 1950's?"

"In this one area, I could handle the 50's. Nothing else – I want to work, I like my independence, and being respected in the workplace, I'm glad I got to play soccer in high school… But knowing for sure that it was the guy's job to ask me out. That I could really get into."

"Wasn't very fair to them though."

"And that's my problem…why?"

Kate hit Clare on the shoulder — and gave her a hug as she hopped out of the car, to fly back to her regular life.

# Chapter 36

Clare expected an uneventful workday on Thursday. She didn't get it. Susan from Shepherd's Center called to say she didn't understand the journal entries Clare's firm had told her to make. Clare felt nervous about asking Pete if she could go over to help. After all, the firm would never really get paid for the time. But Pete surprised her by saying, "In the long run, it makes more sense for you to help her now, so we don't have to write off so much time next year."

Once Clare showed Susan how to make the entries, she wanted to do it herself, with Clare watching and checking her work. Clare went into daydream mode – until she recognized the man from Starbucks, the counselor coming in, and it brought back all her questions about his relationship with Gus. What was the deal with this guy?

Susan noticed her stare, and whispered, "Yeah, he's pretty good looking, isn't he?"

Clare felt her face getting red.

Susan continued, "He's married though, although nobody has ever met his wife."

Considering that she'd never met the spouse of half her co-workers, she didn't really think much of that, but it was clear Susan thought it was weird.

After he went upstairs, Clare said, "So, is he the office mystery man? Phantom wife, checks made out to strangers?"

"I guess he is. I mean he's totally a nice guy, and he seems to be a very popular counselor, but he sure does keep his private life private." She finished her sentence in a whisper, and Clare looked around reflexively to see if someone else was nearby. Her phone went off, alerting her to a text from Paul. "Attorney says he has something for us. Can you meet me at his office at 4:00?" Looking at her watch she saw she had enough time to get across town, if Susan finished the entries in the next twenty minutes, so she texted back, "See you there."

"Everything okay?" Susan asked.

"I hope so." She'd been trying not to think about Maria – since it just made her frustrated and upset every time she did. No clue in Paul's text about whether this was going to be good or bad news. He probably didn't know either.

Without the chatting, Susan finished quickly, and Clare was able to leave just in time. She pulled up in front of the lawyer's office, lucked out with a parking place, and found Paul waiting in the outer office.

"We're next," he said.

They went into the office, to see the attorney's desk just as full of files as the last time. He looked up at them and pulled from the pile.

"Okay – I think Maria's got a good chance. Nobody wants to see these kids become wards of the state, and she doesn't have any record, so people are talking to me about plea bargains that could end with a good result. Nothing's in the bag, of course, and I'll need sworn statements from the two of you about her character."

Paul said, "I'll be glad to do that, even though I haven't known her for that long. But Clare's known her a little longer, so hopefully that will help."

The lawyer gave them each a sheet with directions about what he wanted. "Here's the odd part," he went on. "Remember how I said, we had to find the husband, or at least be sure no one else knew something about him that we didn't?"

"Yes."

"Well, I hire private detectives all the time to do my work. But this time, a friend of mine asked me to reach out to this guy I used to use, and so I decided to do that for this case, because I didn't think my normal guys were available for out of town work. So, anyway I got in touch with him through this old friend, and the guy took one look at the name and said he'd take the case for expenses. No fee."

"Why would he do that?"

"I asked him if he knew the family or something, but he wouldn't say anything. I used to use him years ago, and he was really good. Totally discreet."

"Well, I guess its good news for us that he doesn't want a fee."

"Yup, just expenses to get down to Immokalee and look around down there."

"Why Immokalee?"

"That part of Florida has had some pretty horrendous history, in terms of how migrant workers get treated. There have even been a couple of slavery cases coming out of there."

Clare felt an involuntary shiver go through her body.

She noticed a strange look on Paul's face. She couldn't identify it, but she could tell something was off. He said, "Well, thanks for the update. Let us know as things progress, and we'll get those sworn statements for you right away."

"I need them before Wednesday. That's when I have a conference with the A.D.A.'s office set up."

Paul and Clare walked out of the office, and as soon as the door closed behind them, he said, "Did you see that?"

"See what?"

"The envelope on his desk. The one he touched when he was talking about the private detective's expenses."

"Not really. What about it?'

"There was a name on the envelope. I read it upside down."

"And?"

"The name on the envelope was Gus Andrews."

# Chapter 37

Gus. Gus – a private detective?  Gus, who seemed so innocent, so honest. Granted her view of private detectives was based solely upon television, but innocent and honest were definitely not words that she would have used to characterize that particular profession. How could Gus be leading a secret life like this?  Clare wanted to tell Paul he was wrong. But she didn't, because she knew things about Gus already that Paul didn't know. Like the money from the counselor. And the meeting he'd obviously been having with that same counselor in Starbucks a few days ago.

So, was Gus some sort of undercover homeless person? That just didn't add up. No one would spend all their time on the streets, just to keep their private detective work secret. And what about how scared he was in the hospital, that they would put him away some place?  If he was undercover, he wouldn't have been so afraid.

On the other hand, she couldn't deny the obvious. Gus wouldn't charge to look for Maria's husband. Not to mention the fact that Gus wouldn't charge if he somehow knew the money was coming from her.

Finally, she looked up at Paul, and said, "I don't get it – but at the same time I think it's true. I think Gus is the one looking for Maria's husband. Do you think he's in danger?"

"Maybe. Immokalee's not exactly Disneyworld."

"So, do we say something to him?"

"That I don't know. It sounds like we might not see him for a few days – if he's on his way down there. We can think about how to handle this. All I know for sure is, Gus isn't who I thought he was."

"Who did you think Gus was?"

"I thought he was a nice old guy, who probably lost his family to some tragic accident, and snapped. I figured he just stopped caring about the way the world thought he should be living, kind of opted out, and survived on a day to day basis, because he didn't want to think about the past."

"Wow! So, do you have theories like that about everybody whose story you don't know?"

"Kind of. I've probably thought more about Gus, with the hospital thing, and the way he's such a presence around here - but yeah – I do do that. It helps me not ask questions I don't have a right to ask. Turns out I'm a really curious person, and if I don't make up the back story, I'm too tempted to cross the boundaries with people."

Silently, Clare thought – who would have guessed that a guy like Paul would be so curious that he had to come up with his own stories?  Every stereotype she'd ever heard was about women having that kind of curiosity. She kind of liked the idea though. Made him seem more real, more human. Which made her think she hadn't gotten to know him well enough yet, because there was probably a lot more real where that came from.

"So, you don't do that?  Am I totally weird?"

"Well, me not doing that doesn't make you totally weird. And I do wonder about people. Sometimes it does take a lot for me not to ask the questions. Especially, I've wondered about Gus. He doesn't fit, somehow. But truthfully, this detective thing doesn't help me very much. He still doesn't make sense to me."

"At least the Maria news was good."

"Yeah – I'm wondering if she knows much about what's happening."

"Did you check out what you'd have to do to see her?"

"I started, but I didn't get too far in making a plan to make it happen."

"Want to go over to Manna House with me, and we'll check it out on the computer together?"

Clare hesitated. She did want to do that. But she was beginning to wonder whether they were destined to be friends who tried to make the world a better place.  Not that there was anything wrong with that. It's just that – she had more feelings for him than that. Or at least she thought she might.

But saying no – that just wasn't an option she could imagine taking.

"Yeah – I have some time. Let's go."

Manna House was empty, of course. Too early for any volunteers to have shown up. There wasn't even a line in front yet. On a beautiful day like this, people wouldn't come until just before dinner.

Paul headed toward the library. He'd put a table in there that he was using as a desk, and he pulled a laptop out from a locked cabinet that looked like a closed-up bookcase. She realized he'd subtly turned the space into an office, without totally taking it over. It made her like him more, if that was possible. She only hoped she wouldn't show her emotions in some embarrassing way.

"So, let's see. They said the center was called Glades, right?"

"Yes. The website is right here." She leaned over and typed the address in.

"Okay. And did you find where it said how you visit people?"

Clare leaned over again, to point out the tab. When she did, she felt Paul's hand on her waist. She didn't lean all the way back to her seat, letting him guide her close enough to see the screen. They kept working on the search, but she wasn't really able to concentrate. When they found the contact info, Paul saved it, and said, "So, the next visitation day for Maria's group is Saturday. They have hours from 8-10, 12-4, and 6:30-8:30. I have to be here, all day – but maybe you could go when you get off work?  That is you could go if you had a valid I.D and a clean record. So, maybe that means you can't go after all." Paul teased.

"Excuse me. Exactly what are you insinuating?" She turned toward him.

"I'm insinuating that you may have something to hide." His voice was still laughing, but it had intensity too.

"No – nothing to hide from you." Clare knew she was jumping from the safety of friendship. If he backed away – she'd be devastated. But risking devastated rather than letting the moment go – she felt like she had to do it or regret not doing it forever.

Paul looked toward the windows. The blinds were closed. He turned Clare toward him, and very softly he began to kiss her. And then harder. And then his hands were on her back, and they were running down her spine, and he was pulling her even closer, and then – someone knocked at the door. Not the library door, thank God. The outside door. They broke apart and tried to look as if nothing had been going on. Paul went to unlock the door.

Gus was standing on the other side.

# Chapter 38

"Clare, I didn't expect to see you here."

"We were just…" She broke off, realizing she didn't want to explain herself at this moment. She wanted Gus to tell them what he was doing here.

"Clare's working with me on a project Gus. Is there something you were looking for from me?" Someone who knew Paul better would have realized he was a little flushed and he was speaking too fast, but his voice sounded normal enough for Gus to take his invitation and start talking.

"Actually, I'm glad you're both here. I wanted to let you know that I'm going out of town for a few days. I didn't want you to worry." Gus directed the last part toward Clare.

"Okay. Thanks for telling us Gus. Is everything okay?"

"Yes. I think so. But I did want to give you this envelope."

"Okay." He handed something to Paul, and Paul read the outside, then looked up, clearly disturbed.

"What is this Gus?"

"It's just in case. I don't think you'll need to open it, but I'd appreciate it if you do if it comes to that. I wasn't sure who to give it to, and then I thought of you and Clare."

Clare was feeling confused by their conversation. Paul handed her the envelope, and she read, 'open if I don't come back' printed on the outside, and then signed by Gus.

"What? Gus, do you think you're not coming back?"

"No – no I think everything will be fine. But a long time ago, I was taught to be prepared for anything. It's just that for these last years, I haven't had a way to really do that. I was thinking about what you said to me the other day Clare. That we are friends, and I realized I should trust you.

"Can you trust me…us… enough to tell us what's going on Gus?"

"Well - all I will say is that I'm going to try to help Maria. It's better if you don't know details. I guess I want you to trust me about that."

"Okay Gus." Paul answered him quickly. "We won't ask questions you don't want us to ask. And we won't open this unless we don't hear from you in... how many days?"

"Well, I'll definitely be back in five days. If I'm not, then something's wrong, and you should read what I wrote. It might be important for somebody else."

Clare could tell that what he was telling them wasn't for his own good. The envelope must have information about Maria's husband.

"Gus, is there anything else we can do to help you with whatever's going on?"

"Can I take some food for the road?"

"Sure – let's go make some sandwiches. And I think there are water bottles in the back too." Clare motioned for Paul to let her go alone with Gus. She figured there'd be a better chance he'd talk to her if they were alone.

"Thanks Clare – you too Paul. I know none of this is part of how things are supposed to be done around here."

She started putting ham slices on top of a piece of bread, leaving out the mayo, to make the sandwich last longer. "So, are you scared about this trip?"

"Maybe a little. But I'm also excited. I'm hoping that whatever I find will make somebody else's life better – a lot better. It's worth the risk."

Clare could see by Gus' eyes that he was telling the truth. He was 100% there, more than she ever remembered seeing him.

Clare put her hand on his shoulder, and said, "Gus, Have a good trip." It felt like more than good wishes. It felt like a blessing.

The two of them went back to Paul. Gus and Paul exchanged a few words – then he left.

"What did he say to you?" Clare asked.

"Just thanks. I told him I'd be praying for him, and he said thanks."

"Should we be doing anything else, do you think?"

"I think we've got to believe he knows what he's doing. But if he's not back in five days – my answer will change."

Clare thought about where they'd been before Gus came in. The moment was broken, but at least she didn't need to worry anymore that they would get stuck in "the friend zone."

"Earth to Clare." Paul was standing close beside her, smiling at her distracted expression.

"Not to be a nag, but it's Thursday night, and Manna House needs its team leader to get to work."

Pretending to punch him lightly on the shoulder, Clare said, "Who do you think you are, my boss or something?"

"Somehow, I have the feeling that's a mistake I better never make."

The group at the door was starting to form, and Clare went quickly over to start setting up. It was Thursday night - the night when she could put everything away, and just be in the moment, the rhythm of Manna House.

# Chapter 39

Clare set her alarm really early on Saturday morning, thinking that if she got to work early, she could put in her required hours, and still get to Glades detention center by 7:30, to see Maria before it closed. After her workday was over, she drove several hours into the middle of the state, over roads most people who visited Florida didn't travel. She went straight to the building with the cement walls and the guard at the gate. The guard directed her to an office with a mini-version of airport security, metal detectors and double thick doors.

Once she got through, Clare saw a room full of waiting people. She was the only one with blonde hair, and she sat down uncomfortably conscious that she didn't fit. People were speaking very fast Spanish all around, except for the ones who were speaking something else – Arabic maybe?  She didn't understand anybody, and just tried to blend into the furniture, wishing she'd brought a book. This looked to be a long wait.

Or so she thought.

"Ms. Wheeler, come over here."

Clare approached the man who'd called her name. "This way," he said.

Clare glanced around the room, wondering why she was going before everybody else. Maybe they hadn't filled out the right paperwork?

Or maybe there was another reason Clare didn't want to think about. She followed the man, who was clearly the authority in this situation. He took her to a room that said Interview 7 on the door and motioned toward it. "She's in there. You have half-an-hour. I'll knock when it's time for you to go."

"Thanks!" Clare said, smiling, in case that somehow helped Maria at a later date. She opened the door to find Maria sitting in a chair on the other side of a table. She was thinner – which seemed strange, since most of her meals before she came to this place had been at shelters. As soon as she saw Clare, her eyes filled with tears.

"Clare!  They didn't tell me who was here. I'm so glad to see you."

Clare realized she was crying too. She went around the table to hug Maria, half-expecting some watching voice to tell her to stay on her side of the table, but thankfully that didn't happen. "How are you Maria? Are you okay in here?"

"I'm just so scared all the time. I can't sleep, I can't eat — I'm just so scared."

Clare was afraid to ask, but she couldn't not ask. "Maria, where are the kids?"

"They're here. They sleep in a children's section, but during the day they are with me. But, you know they are citizens of the U.S., so if they deport me, they still don't deport the kids."

"Could you take them with you? I mean, I hope that doesn't happen, but if it does, can you take them home with you?"

"I don't know if I really should. When I was growing up it was so beautiful, so many cousins and friends to run and play with. But I left because there was no life for me back home anymore. No way to make money, and too many drug wars breaking out in the streets. I don't want them to have that kind of life. I'm not even sure how that would work. They wouldn't be deported, and I can't pay for plane tickets — I don't know. But I'm most scared about Roberto. If we have to leave, how will he ever find us?"

"So, you think he's still alive." She'd never been sure what Maria really thought.

Maria went on, "I think if he was dead. I would feel it. Feel the emptiness. But I don't. I just feel like he's away, and he'll be back, and I want him to be able to find me when he comes back."

Then she stopped herself, saying, "I'm sorry, I should have started by telling you thank you for Manna House helping me get a lawyer. Most of the people here feel like they don't have a chance, they just wish the waiting was over, but I don't feel that way. Having the lawyer makes me think I have a chance."

"How are the kids coping with being cooped up in here?"

"You'd be surprised how strong kids can be. They keep trying to make the best of it. We're on an adventure, that's what Paola says. And there are books, and a little playground. I'm trying to be grateful for what we have."

"How are the people that work here? How do they treat you?"

The way she looked around, Clare felt like Maria was telling her to be careful what she said. Could the room be bugged?

That seemed crazy – but who knows?  It was possible that some of the people who ended up in this center could know something that the government wanted to know.

"It's fine."  She stopped there - and Clare didn't ask for more.

"Many of the people here are very nice."  She said with a slight smile. She had used her English precisely and well.

"How are the rest of the people at Manna House?"  They talked for a while, sharing the news from the outside world that had been her community for so long. Clare didn't say a word about Gus. She was worried about how Maria would feel if she knew about his trip. Then a knock came at the door, and Clare got up immediately to leave, not wanting to do anything that would cause negative attention to come Maria's way.

"Thank you, Clare. Thanks for coming."

"Give the kids my love."

"I will."

"I'll see you again." Clare said. Now that she'd been here once, the hurdle of her nervousness was over. And who knows? Maybe the fact that Maria had guests would help make sure the "Many of the people who are nice," would be sure to be careful to treat Maria well. People say that's how nursing homes work – the more people come to visit – the more the workers pay attention to the patient. Maybe detention centers worked the same way.

Maria had tears in her eyes as she turned to go, and so did Clare. She drove home praying for strength for Maria and the kids, for Gus, for all of them.

# Chapter 40

Sunday gave Clare a chance to catch up on her sleeping as well as on her laundry. She'd been thinking about going to church and decided it might be a good thing to do that night, particularly when she had so much to pray about.

As she entered, she involuntarily looked around, as if she might know someone there. It was strange, but she had this odd feeling that Paul might show up. Which didn't even make sense, since he'd be busy at Manna House right now. Just wishful thinking, because she wanted to see him. Lost in those thoughts, she wasn't aware of anyone around her, until she felt a tap on the shoulder.

It was Velma! Clare almost jumped in her seat. Velma didn't say a word, but Clare could feel her nervousness, and she motioned that Velma could sit with her. The room was silent, which felt strange in a way. Sitting next to someone she knew, but not saying a word.

She closed her eyes to pray, for Maria, for Gus, for Kate and her exams, for Velma who had found her way to this room tonight, and then she found herself praying for Paul. She wondered what he would have thought of that if he'd known.

The music, the candles, the scripture readings, they all fed her. She definitely felt more at peace than before, not even wondering why Paul hadn't called since Thursday night – well hardly wondering at all. But Velma, Clare could see she was having trouble with the quiet. She wasn't looking fed, she was looking terrified.

They walked out together – and the silence lasted for a few more moments. Finally, Velma said, "I guess it's kind of weird for you that I showed up here. It's just that I saw a sign." She stopped talking then, as if whatever she was going to say next would have been too personal for her to share. "I'm sorry if you feel like I've intruded on your place." She looked really disturbed.

"No – no. This is no more my place than anybody else's." Clare looked at her and tried to think of what to say to help take away some of the discomfort. "Really – I'm glad you found your way here."

And then it hit her. Didn't A.A. meet in churches sometimes? Maybe that was the sign that Velma saw? Glancing down the hallway, Clare saw people on their way to a room at the end of a corridor. Could that be a meeting room?

Clare silently prayed again, "Please God – please let her find the help she needs. Please".

Finally, she just said – "Velma, This was exactly the place I wanted to be tonight, and I'm glad you were here too." Then she left, hoping to give Velma a chance to go to a meeting, if that's what she was looking for. Clare resisted the impulse to look back and see if Velma made her way down the hall. She just kept praying and hoping that whatever had gotten Velma through the door in the first place would lead her to the recovery she needed.

When she got home, there was a message on the machine. Clare listened, hoping it would be from Paul, and it was. Only it wasn't at all what she wanted to hear.

"Hey Clare. I'm just calling because I got a weird hang-up at Manna House, and the Caller I.D. said Immokalee. I wouldn't have expected a call from Gus, but I don't know anyone else who would be calling from down there. He didn't leave a message, which is making me even more crazy. Anyway, I just wanted to say this out loud to somebody. I know you're probably busy. You don't have to call me back, but if you want to, use my cell number, because by the time you get this, I'll probably be gone from Manna House."

Clare's imagination began immediately going wild. She could picture Gus at a pay phone trying to tell them he was in danger, and some stranger hanging up the phone on him. Then she listened to the message again and realized that Paul was expecting her not to get the message until really late. Right now, he'd still be at Manna House. She put her inhibitions aside, got in the car, and drove over. She wanted to hear Paul say that he thought everything was okay, that she was going overboard. From his message, it sounded like he was hoping for the same thing from her. They might not do each other much good, but at least they'd have an over-active imagination together.

Clare pulled into the parking lot, and judging by the people moving out the door, she was just in time to help with clean up.

Who cares if Paul hadn't asked her out, she was here now, and she was here because it was where she needed to be, whether he liked it or not.

"Clare!  Oh man, I'm sorry. I must have scared you with my message."

"It's okay – I'm glad you called – but I am worried. I think it's really strange that Gus would call. And doubly strange that he would start to call, and then hang up"

"I know. I have this gut feeling that he's in trouble. I know he said we should wait five days before panicking, but I'm already there."

"Well, if you count the day he left as one, Friday as two – then we're on four – and it's after five – so we're really close to five days."

"That's an interesting counting system you've got there."

"I'm the one people come to when they want to rationalize doing something. I can always think of a way to make things seem like they're okay. Granted, that's not necessarily a good character trait – it's just who I am."

Paul started to laugh. "I can see that's a trait that could come in handy!  Especially if Gus gets angry at us for breaking his confidence."

"Sounds like you're thinking of opening that envelope."

"I am. I want to know if he wrote anything about where he is."

"But what if it's not that?  What if it's his story – you know – next of kin – that kind of information."

"Maybe we could skim for information we need, and not let ourselves look closely at anything that doesn't pertain to Immokalee?"

"I guess we could do that – or at least try to do that. It's shaky – but it might work."  Clare thought for a minute, then said, "You know there was a time when I wouldn't have tried to do that. If there's anyone whose story I really want that I don't have it's Gus. But now – I don't want it, if he doesn't want to give it to me. And I certainly don't want it because we think Gus is in danger. So, I'm convinced – we should open it. We're doing it for the right reasons."

"All right, as soon as all the volunteers leave, we'll look at it. I don't want to take a chance of anyone else seeing anything."

They both went to work helping to clean up. Looking around, Clare didn't see anyone besides the volunteer group helping. "Where's the Sunday night host? Trish, isn't it?"

"Yeah, she asked to leave early. I told her I'd cover – but I knew that meant I'd be working even later than usual. I gave her the night to have plans, which meant I couldn't have any." Clare realized that last part was probably for her benefit. Telling her why he hadn't called to set up a late date for tonight. It didn't help much actually. She still didn't understand why he hadn't called for Friday, or for Saturday. And it wouldn't have been that late for him, if he'd had to clean up on his own. It's not like they were old people. They could start an evening after nine o'clock.

She went into the kitchen to help the group clean up. She suddenly didn't want to be right beside Paul, while she was thinking these negative things about him. 'You are here for Gus – that's what you are doing here. Focus,' she told herself. And it worked, because she really was there for Gus, her friend who might be in danger.

Once the volunteers left, they went to his office. He pulled out the envelope, and without hesitating again, opened the seal. Clare waited as he skimmed the first page, looked at the second, and quickly went back to the first.

"On the first page, he tells us he's in Immokalee looking for Maria's husband. He wrote down where he was going to start the search. Some kind of coalition group that he was going to talk to. He said they helped break up a slavery ring a few years ago."

"A few years ago? I heard the lawyer say that - but I can't believe it. I feel like we're talking about a few hundred years ago."

"No, I remember reading about it. These people brought immigrants in, telling them their paperwork was good, and then once they got here, they held them prisoner, telling them that they didn't have legal paperwork, and they'd have to work for free for them to earn it. It only got discovered because somebody finally escaped."

"Does Gus say why he's looking there for Maria's husband?"

"He says he talked to somebody who said her husband told him he was going to take a risk to find work a few years back – and the job he was looking at was in Immokalee."

He gestured to the other page. "This is the one we don't want to read, that explains what to do if he doesn't make it. Who to contact, that kind of stuff. And there's a note to you in it too. It looks like it's an explanation of some kind."

"I'm not going to read that. Not yet. I hope not ever."

"Okay. Well from this note, we know at least where he started the search – with this coalition group. What do we do with that?"

"I could call out for tomorrow. I could drive down to Immokalee, look around, see if I could find him." Clare said it with confidence, hoping she was covering up the fear she was feeling.

"Oh great. So, you'll do that, give me a letter, and five days from now, I'll be on my own, wondering whether to open it or not. I don't think so."

"So, what's your idea?" Fine to shoot hers down – but there had to be an alternative she was willing to agree to, or she was going whether he liked it or not.

"I'm going."

"You have to work."

"I'll call a board member. I'm not supposed to be working seven days a week you know. I've just been doing that so I could get to know everybody. It's time for me to take them at their word, and take some time off."

"Well, the nightly hosts did used to get by without you, ya know."

"I know, I know. And I'm sure they did an awesome job. And my job isn't to do their job. Geez, haven't we talked about this before?"

Clare realized they both were getting testy now. Which made sense – they were worried, and maybe a little guilty, since, Gus wouldn't be in whatever situation he was in if they hadn't gotten this whole thing started.

"Okay." Clare said. "We're both going. That's the only answer that will satisfy both of us, and maybe it will actually be helpful to have two brains trying to figure out what's going on."

"You know he could be fine. You realize that."

"I do. I think he is fine. I'm even thinking we should get in touch with the Monday night host and have them call us when Gus shows up for the evening meal."

"But just in case…"

"Just in case he doesn't, we'll already be in Immokalee, getting the lay of the land, and figuring out where he is, so that we can bring him home."

Paul looked as if he didn't want to say whatever he was thinking. Clare just stayed quiet, and finally he said, "This sounds like more than a one-day trip."

"Maybe. We could drive back and forth – it's only a couple of hours. And if I have to call in for a few days, I have personal time."

"Didn't you already take that when Gus was in the hospital?"

"Okay – I'll take vacation time. It's not like I need to travel anywhere. After all, we already live in paradise."

Paul laughed at her attempt to lighten the atmosphere. "All right. I guess I'll let you figure your life out. It's going to be complicated enough figuring out my own."

Clare walked toward the door. "Tomorrow then?"

"Tomorrow. I'll pick you up at 7:30 A.M.- that is if you don't mind taking my car."

"We can take your car. I'm fine with that." She left, quick to go out before him, quick to make sure the date he hadn't asked for didn't materialize because she was in the right place at the right time. Clare didn't want any more dates that weren't intentional. Whatever came next with Paul was going to be because he asked her out and she said yes. And in the meantime, she was prepared to be friends on a mission, on the way to finding Gus.

# Chapter 41

The alarm went off, and this morning Clare knew exactly where she was. The night before, she'd been trying and trying to come up with a plan. What did they think they were doing?  It was pretty crazy, just wandering into territory where they had reason to believe Gus might be in trouble. Problem was, they couldn't not do it. Something was calling her to get in the car, and just go. Just show up.

Once, a long time ago, her folks were getting ready to go to a funeral. Clare and Kate hadn't wanted to go. They were afraid they wouldn't know what to say. And her Mom said, "It's not about what you say. It's about showing up. That's what we do in this family. We show up."

So, in this situation, that's the best advice Clare could lay her hands on. Showing up. Showing up for a friend. Trusting that that would be enough, the way it had seemed to be enough so many years ago.

The analogy worked, except she didn't like that it was the memory of a family friend's death that was giving it to her. That wasn't what this was, Clare told herself, believing it, at least for now.

Paul looked to Clare as if he was in the same contemplative mood she was in, when he came to her door. They walked to the car in silence, but it wasn't awkward. It was intense.

Getting in and starting the car, Paul started talking, "Clare, I've been thinking off and on all night, trying to figure out a plan."

"Does that mean you didn't sleep?  Maybe I should drive."

"No – I slept – but then I'd wake up, with an idea. I finally got up and put a pencil and paper by my bed, in case something brilliant came to me, so I wouldn't forget it in the morning."

"Well – did anything brilliant come to you?"

"The best I had was what we already talked about. Going to the Coalition. But you know what I realized?  We don't even have a picture to flash around."

"Yeah – that's true. Manna House isn't really a place people take pictures, and even if it was – I can't see Gus ever having let himself be in one."

"Do you remember what he was wearing the day he left? Not that he was necessarily wearing that – but I don't know. I'm grasping at straws now."

"No that's a good idea. Haven't you ever noticed, Gus wears the same clothes all the time?  Same shirt, same pants, topped off with his grey sweater."

They spent awhile, listing the things they could think of that would help somebody know if they'd ever seen Gus. Clare typed the list into her phone – so they wouldn't forget the slightest detail.

"Okay, so we go to the coalition, we see if they tell us anything. Then what?" Paul still sounded really stressed out. Clare knew they were entering into a tough situation, but it surprised her that she seemed to be the calm one.

"Well, the town itself isn't that big, according to what I found on-line. You know what we should have done?  We should have looked up to see if there was some version of Manna House there. I would think there has to be something, with all the poverty I've read about in Immokalee."

"So – how much of a smart phone is that that you're holding?  Do you think you could find what we need on it?"

"Sure, no problem."  Clare's Dad always told her to only buy the plan you need, so her data portion wasn't very big, but she didn't share that with Paul. The cell phone bill would just have to go over budget for the month. Her checking account would survive.

"Here it is. The Guadalupe Center. Says it started in the 1980's to help the migrant workers in the area. Now they are into education and growth, but they still serve 35000 hot meals a year. Wow. How many meals do we serve at Manna House?"

"I think the paperwork the board showed me was closer to 50000."

"Seriously?  I'm an accountant, but apparently, I'm not as good at numbers as I would have thought. I never would have come up with that high of a guess."

"Well, when you do seven days a week, it adds up pretty quickly. At any rate, it sounds like this Guadalupe Center is a pretty big place. If Gus was hungry, I bet he'd find it."

"So, we have a plan B now. We go to the Coalition, and if they don't have anything to tell us, we go over to the Guadalupe Center."

"I like it." Paul did look more relaxed, which was good to see. "So, Clare, did you call your boss? I was thinking about it - isn't this your busiest time of the year?"

"I got up early, and wrote an email to my supervisor, Pete before he would have gotten to the office. He's a really great guy, so I think he'll be okay with it. And truthfully, I would have been useless at work if I didn't come with you. What did you tell the Board about leaving town? Did you tell them anything specific?"

"I just told them I needed the day off. I called the President, and she was great. She said, "We're the ones who've been telling you not to work a seven-day week. Take the time you need. She didn't ask any questions."

He went on, "I called Andrea, because she's the one scheduled to run dinner today. I told her that I had to go out of town, and then I asked her if she could call my cell if Gus happened to come in. She didn't ask any questions either, which was good, because I didn't know what I was going to tell her if she did."

They got quiet for a minute, and then another minute. Clare looked out the window, noticing the exit signs, and as she saw the mileage for Naples was getting smaller, she felt a tightness begin to fill up her chest. She was scared. Scared for herself, scared for Gus. And then, she remembered that this all started because of Maria, and her family. Maria must have been so terrified over the years, wondering where this man she loved had gone. She must have felt so helpless. And now, things were even worse. Now, the life she'd had was gone, and she had no clue what was coming next. Thinking about Maria helped Clare breathe again. Whatever they were doing, they were doing for the right reasons. Maria was worth it. Gus knew that, Paul knew that – and Clare knew that.

# Chapter 42

The Coalition offices were actually pretty nice. The building kind of reminded Clare of New Mexico. Everything there was Adobe Brown, with flowering trees around – and that's what this building looked like. In good shape, compared to its neighborhood, with nice landscaping too. Across the street was a large parking lot; from what she'd been reading that made sense. The coalition had placed themselves right where people were picked up for work every morning. That way, people could come and talk if they needed to, and still get a day's labor when the growers came. Clare remembered reading about boycotts that were going on – so it wasn't surprising to see signs that said 'Fair Food' and 'Soy humano.' Clare figured these were the signs they carried outside of the restaurants and grocery stores they were picketing. From what she'd read, the people who picked the food in the fields were paid almost nothing - like $40 a day for picking and carrying 2000 pounds of tomatoes. It made her so sad to think that the people who put food on her table were treated as less than human.

As someone approached them, Paul nodded for Clare to speak. In all their plan making, they hadn't rehearsed this part.

"We're looking for our friend." Clare said. "We think he might be in trouble, or maybe hurt – or maybe he's just fine – but we want to know."

"Did your friend say he was coming here?" The man's voice wasn't rude, but he wasn't friendly either.

"That's what he said. He was looking for somebody too."

"Okay." The man either didn't understand, or at least wasn't helping her fill in the blanks in her conversation.

Paul said, "Clare, maybe it would help if we tell him what our friend looks like."

She looked down at the list on her phone, and began to read it to him. "Six two, Caucasian, 200 lbs. About fifty years old, white hair, blue eyes." When she glanced up, he had a small smile on his face.

"Well, in this area, that man might have stuck out a little." Clare had noticed on the way into town that most of the people on the street appeared to be Latino men – Latino young men, so she understood the smile.

"But I'm sorry. I can't help you." He said.

"You can't help me? Does that mean you haven't seen my friend?"

Clare saw a look of understanding pass over Paul's face. She wondered what he was seeing that she wasn't.

"Okay – thanks anyway. Let's go Clare."

As soon as they were out the door, Paul said, "We can't go at it this way. Man, I hope we didn't blow it already. People are going to think we're here to cause trouble. They are probably used to immigration officers, or undercover police. This isn't the kind of town you can just walk around asking questions in."

"That makes sense. So, what do we do?"

"What if we go over to that Guadalupe Center, and just ask them to show us around? Tell them we're from Manna House, see if we can get some common ground."

"And then what?'

"I don't know. I'm flying blind here. I guess I'm just hoping for a plan to develop as we go along."

"Do you think this guy will call people and tell them not to help us?"

"I hope not, but I guess it's possible. Who knows how the communication network runs around here."

"All right – well if that might happen, let's get over to Guadalupe Center right away. It's only a few blocks from here. If we're already there as representatives from Manna House – they might not jump to the conclusion that we're the ones he's talking about." Paul was rustling around in his wallet as Clare was talking.

"I found it! The board had cards made up for me as a welcome gift. I can get out a card to start with, so that they'll know we're not lying about who we are. That might make it easier to get some info in the long run."

They'd been walking in the direction her phone told her to go and were almost at Guadalupe Center. It was a pretty impressive looking place. Much more established than Manna House. There was even an office entrance separate from the main door, with a doorbell and an intercom, so that whoever was working could buzz people in when the main program doors weren't open.

When they buzzed, a woman's voice answered. "Can I help you?"

It felt weird talking to a door. "Hi – we're visiting in the area. We're from Manna House up in Sarasota, and we heard about your program. We wondered if we could look around."

The woman hit the buzzer again, this time to let them in.

She came out of her office to greet them, saying, "I don't have anyone to give you a tour right now, but you're welcome to look around. There are people in most of our program areas setting up for the day, so you can ask them questions about what they're doing. They love to talk about their work" She was very friendly. Paul had his card in his hand just in case, but she seemed to trust them. She gave them nametags, so that they'd look official as they wandered around.

She was right too; the place was full of volunteers. Some were in the kitchen, some were sorting in something they called "the clothes closet." It was really a room larger than Clare's apartment living room.

Paul spoke up. "Hi, we're from Manna House in Sarasota. That's quite a pile of clothes you have there."

One of the women looked up. "We get a pile like this at least once a week. A lot of the churches in Naples collect for us. Then about once a week a volunteer drives out bags from each church."

"Do you need that many clothes? Doesn't it get overwhelming?"

"You'd think so, wouldn't you? But there's always new people coming into this community, needing clothes. And we have our regulars too, who come in every so often, when their clothes get worn out."

"Do you have clothes for kids?"

"Sometimes, but we don't have as many kids here as they do up north. Most of the people who come into this area are young men from Central America, looking to make some money, and send it home to their parents, or sometimes their wife and kids."

"And once in a while, we get a homeless person from the U.S. A few years back one of the northern states decided to bus their homeless people to Florida."

"What?" Clare needed her to explain what she'd just said.

"Yeah – they figured at least if the people were here, they wouldn't die of exposure in the winter."

"I can't believe that was a plan."

"I'm sure some politician ran on the "I'll fix the homeless problem," platform. And so, people arrived here, and it is better in the winter. But summer comes, and it's not exactly easy living on these streets in the heat. And – they need different clothes. That's where we come in."

"The strangest case we had lately was a guy who had the right clothes for the weather, except he had a sweater on. He came in asking if we could loan him clothes."

"Yeah," said the other woman. "Never heard that one before. He wanted to leave his old clothes here and wear some new ones for a day or two, then come back and switch back."

Clare looked at Paul, and then said, "That is sort of curious. Did you help him out?"

"Sure. We even washed his stuff for him, so it would be clean when he came back."  She gestured toward the corner of the room when she said that. Clare wandered toward the direction she'd pointed. "Come to think of it, he said he'd be back to get it today."

There, on a shelf by itself was a pile of clothing. On the top, was Gus' sweater.

# Chapter 43

Clare wanted to tell Paul what she'd seen, without raising too much interest in the minds of the clothes closet volunteers. Luckily right then the woman who had let them in came to tell them where they could get a cup of coffee, so they followed her to an area of the kitchen.

"This is the volunteer station," she said. "Some of our volunteers live fairly close and come on a weekly basis. Others come in for a day, just to see what we're doing, where they're sending their donations. We like to say yes to everybody who wants to get involved, because we need the help, and because we want people to see the people who come here are good people. Nothing to be afraid of." She heard a buzz and went to answer it.

"Paul, in that pile the woman pointed to. Gus' sweater was on that pile."

"Are you sure?"

"I'm sure. Gus has had that sweater on just about every time I've seen him, no matter what the weather for as long as I've known him. Why would he take it off?"

"I don't know. Maybe some kind of a disguise? Anyway, the good news is he got here safely. And he's planning on coming back."

"Right. Do you think we should ask those women any more questions?"

"No. I think we were lucky to get all the info we got, without asking any questions. Hopefully, we haven't raised any red flags yet."

"Should we leave, and ask if we can come back at meal time? Tell the woman at the front desk we want to see them in action. If Gus is coming to get his stuff that seems like the time he might do it. Although, I'm not sure what we would do in the meantime?"

"Let's do what we said we were here to do. Let's stay here and look at what this place is doing and figure out if any of it could translate to Manna House."

Clare started with the bulletin board, reading the announcements from Guadalupe Center, and other groups they seemed to have connections with in the area. They had a tutoring program, teaching people English. And they were having some kind of a fund-raiser, which by the size of this place they must need. And even though the woman said most of their clothing needs were adults, there still seemed to be plenty of kids and teenagers that needed help, judging by the pictures of the people on the board.

'Manna House could do some of this,' Clare thought. 'Not exactly the same - but maybe we could have tutoring programs for the kids. Kids like Maria's who didn't have an easy place to lay down and read a book before they went to sleep at night.'

Maria's kids. She'd been thinking about Gus all morning, and how they could make sure he was okay. But now she began to wonder if it was possible that he had found out anything about Maria's husband. The Dad her kids hadn't seen for so long. It seemed impossible that he would find him after all this time. But if he did…it would make everything Maria was going through now worth it to her.

Paul had wandered over to a wall with books and pamphlets. She could see his brain turning, thinking about what they could have in the library at Manna House that would be more helpful than what was there now.

She asked, "Well, do they have ideas here that you think would work for us?"

"Dozens of ideas are coming to my mind. I'm making mental notes."

Just then she heard a sound. Someone was unlocking a door, and Clare realized they must be getting ready for the lunch shift. Paul heard the same sound. They didn't speak; they just looked at each other, and moved toward the back of the room, where they'd have a good view as people came in.

Gus was about the twelfth person to come through the door. He had a hat covering his hair, and part of his face, but Clare still recognized him, and by the slight tension she felt in Paul's posture, she knew he saw him too.

Clare's relief was huge. She realized how much fear had been building up in her, as the emotion tried to come up to the surface. The tears tried to form in her eyes. She wanted to go to

Gus, but before she took a step, he saw them. And the very slight "no" motion he made with his head was unmistakable. They needed to leave – and now.

Paul saw it too. He followed her toward the office.

"Thanks for letting us look around." Clare said. "We got a lot of ideas."

"This place really is doing fantastic work." Paul said.

"Glad you came by."

Back out in the daylight, Clare said, "Man I hope we didn't mess anything up by coming here."

"We did what we felt we had to do. Personally, I still think Gus is in danger, more than we knew when he left to come down here."

"Yeah – but not more than he knew. That's why he came to see us and left us that envelope. He knew what he was doing. And by what I saw in that room, I think he still knows what he's doing."

"So, what are you saying?"

"I'm saying we should get out of his way." Clare said, beginning to pick up that she and Paul might not be on the same page.

"Just leave. That's what you want to do."

"Well, what other ideas do you have? It was clear he didn't want us to approach him, and if we don't approach him, we don't know what he's doing."

"We could try looking around ourselves – I just have a bad feeling." Paul seemed really troubled, but that just frustrated Clare more.

"Of course, you have a bad feeling. There are things here that aren't right – we knew that before we got in the car. But to me it comes down to do we trust Gus or not. If Gus wanted our help, he would have found a way to let us know. He wants us to leave – didn't you see that in that look he gave us? Or did you miss that?"

"I didn't miss it. Obviously, I didn't miss it. I just don't like to think I sent someone into a situation that could get him hurt or worse. And then I turn around and go home to my comfortable apartment as if it none of this is happening. Maybe you have something more important to do, but I'll just be waiting and worrying."

"Are you trying to say I'm putting my work in front of Gus? Because that's totally out of bounds. Seriously, if we don't approach Gus, we don't know what he's doing. And frankly, I think if we interfere, when we don't know what he's doing – we're likely to get him in more trouble, not less."

"So that's what you think of me, that I'm worthless in a crisis?"

Clare kept walking, even faster, as she said, "You know what, this isn't about you at all."

"Then what is it about? The way I see it, we came here to help Gus, and we shouldn't be leaving."

"And the way I see it, we either trust Gus or we don't. Gus told us to leave, and we need to go."

They got to the car, and Paul unlocked the door.

She looked Paul right in the eye. "Look, if you want to stay, you can just drive me to a bus station, and I'll go home that way. I think we'd be putting Gus in danger, and I'm not doing that."

Paul hesitated for a moment more. Than he said, "I guess I don't really know what to do. You're probably right. If we followed Gus, we might be messing up his plans. Okay I guess I'll come back now too." He wasn't happy, but he resigned himself to the situation.

Clare just nodded and got in the car. In the course of ten minutes, she'd felt great joy and relief, fear, and anger. Spending hours in the car with Paul right now didn't feel like something she wanted to do.

She could feel Paul looking at her, but she kept her eyes focused out the window. They'd crossed a line with that argument, and they were both too hurt to get over it right away. "Music?"

"Music is a good idea," Clare said with the calmest tone she could manage.

He took out a C.D. – and they listened to Simon and Garfunkel, letting the words and the music fill the space that had opened up between them.

And then – Paul's cell phone rang. He pulled off the road to answer it – even though they were already on the highway.

"Hello?" He mouthed that it was Gus, and she got out a pen to write anything down he told her. Paul listened for what felt like forever before he spoke again.

"Okay. We can do that. Of course. We'll go to the hotel on the way into town and wait to hear from you. We'll have all the information ready to go." Go to a hotel? What was Gus saying?

Paul hung up. He was quiet for another few seconds, then he said, "I'm going to get off at the exit, so we can talk about what Gus said, and what you want to do."

"All right."

He got off the exit and pulled into a parking lot, then turned to face her.

"Gus says he thinks he's got a lead that might take him to Roberto. It's a long shot, but it's the best he's got, and he says even if the man he finds isn't Roberto – he's somebody's Roberto." Clare nodded solemnly at Gus' words. It sounded exactly like something Gus would say.

"He wants us to stay close with the car, because he might need emergency transportation."

Clare took this in and came to the only conclusion that made any sense. "Gus is saying that he thinks Roberto has been held against his will. That's what you're telling me."

"He doesn't know for sure. He just wants us to be ready." Paul stopped and looked at her again.

"Clare – I can get you home and come right back. I probably never should have gone along with you getting into this in the first place."

"I don't think I gave you a choice. And no, I'm not going home. I'm not going anywhere except, apparently, the Immokalee Inn." She went on, "Paul - look I was never against staying. I was just against getting in Gus's way. I don't get why that made you so angry."

"I just don't like to be in a position where I can't solve a problem. I'm sorry; I shouldn't have taken my frustration out on you."

"Listen Paul - I get that you wanted a job where you could help people in trouble. You're just going to have to get used to the reality that you can't do it all the time for everybody. And you can't do it by yourself." He didn't say anything, but she could tell that he was listening to what she'd said.

Clare opened up the maps app to see the fastest way back to the Immokalee Inn. She put the phone up on the holder on Paul's dashboard, ready to let go of their earlier argument.

And then a text appeared on the screen, right where the directions were supposed to be.

"Hey Clare - can we get together again? I'd love to see you, Danny."

Clare read the words - and was surprised to feel nothing but annoyance. She recognized that the little excitement that had always come along with Danny showing up was finally gone. Clare had no intention of meeting Danny for any reason. He was engaged, he was supposed to move to California, and she was totally, unequivocally done. Clare reached up and deleted the message. But not before Paul had read it - it had been right in his face. He couldn't really help but see it. And then he looked at her - waiting to see what she would say.

"You know - the broken relationship from college that I mentioned?"

"Let me guess - Danny?"

"Yes."

"So, you still see him?"

"No. No!  He's engaged, might even be married by now actually."

"But - you have seen him." Suddenly - Clare felt like she was on trial.

"I saw him a few months ago."  Where was this coming from? That wasn't the place they were in. She wasn't even sure they were actually dating, let alone exclusively dating. "You know - this conversation doesn't really feel right to me. I don't think I have to tell you about who I've seen or who I haven't seen."

"Okay - then don't."  He was angry - there was no mistaking that tone of voice.

"Listen - maybe the stress is getting to both of us - let's just stop talking before we say something we wish we didn't."

"That sounds like a good plan." And they drove silently to the Inn.

# Chapter 44

When they went to the desk to check-in, Clare was half afraid that this would turn into a scene from a bad movie, with only one room available. But the highway two-story motel, that seemed to be really made for truck drivers, had plenty of room for them. The clerk did give them rooms next to each other, and a funny look, since they were checking in without bags - but Clare just put what she might be thinking out of her head.

At 8:30 she realized she really needed to call Pete at home. She figured he'd be in a pretty relaxed mood at that point. Kids in bed – ready to watch a basketball game on T.V. She was hoping for a quick 'no problem.'

"You're what? You're not coming in tomorrow? You can't do that."

"Pete calm down. There's nothing for you to raise your voice about. There's nothing urgent on my desk."

"Listen Clare – did you never read your contract? You can't take any days off between February 15th and April 15th. No exceptions. When I got your e-mail this morning – I put your stuff around on your desk, so that people would think you were around somewhere – but that's not going to work a second day. One of the partners already came by twice, as if he had a sense something was weird."

"That's crazy. I mean – thanks for covering for me. I didn't mean to put you in that position. But what do you mean we can't take days off for those two months. What if I get sick?"

"Are you sick?" He was calmer now.

"No."

"Are you sure? I think I hear hoarseness in your voice. Yup – I bet you've got a fever."

"Look Pete, I appreciate the effort – but really I don't want to lie about this. A friend is in trouble and I need to be here."

"Where's here?"

"Immokalee."

"Immokalee? What kind of friend are you involved with way down there?"

"A good friend. One of the best people I know."

"Well does this good friend understand that you've got less than a 50:50 chance of keeping your job if you don't come in tomorrow?"

She thought about how upset both Gus and Paul would be if they knew that. But Clare felt strangely calm, like whatever happens happens.

"Okay Pete, you've given me fair notice. If anything happens to me it's not your fault. Okay?"

"Not okay – but I guess I don't get a vote. Listen Clare, whatever you are up to, be careful."

"Okay." She hung up quickly, while Pete was in a relatively calm mood.

The phone rang and checking the number she could see it was Kate.

Trying to sound normal, Clare asked, "Hey, how did the exams go?"

"They were rough, to tell you the truth. But I felt as prepared as I could have been. So, I'm trying to let it go."

"And how does a law school student let it go these days?"

"At the moment, she calls her sister to vicariously experience a love life she doesn't have. Me and the dog guy are history."

"Well, if that were true, it would pretty much be the first time I've had more going on than you."

"Please."

"Anyway – I haven't been out with anybody."

"Yeah? Then why haven't I been able to get you lately?"

"Well it wasn't because I was having romantic evenings."

"Don't tell me. It's something to do with Manna House, but not official dates."

"You're right. Actually, I'm not too sure if I'll be having any more dates of any kind with Paul."

"What are you talking about? You guys seemed like you were made for each other."

Kate couldn't see Clare's glance toward the hotel room wall, where she knew Paul was on the other side.

Kate paused, and when Clare didn't say anything she went on. "So, what about Paul? To tell you the truth, I left Florida thinking you'd found the man for you."

"Paul is pretty great. But I don't like how he doesn't make an effort to see me. I know he's busy, and I know there are lots of new things happening in his life, but I don't like the sense that he doesn't think about me at all when we're not together. All our dates come out of times he sees me, and then makes a plan."

"Is that true?"

"It might be a little harsh, but yeah that's what I've been feeling. He didn't call me for this weekend at all, until something came up with Gus."

"Well, yeah, but you guys seemed so in sync. Same things important to both of you. Same vision. Plus, he's really good looking. Not that that matters, of course." She started laughing, remembering that they always said that at the end of any evaluation of somebody's looks. Their parents raised them to be deeper than judging people by their looks – but hey they were only human.

"So, Clare – what about Maria? Any word on her?"

"The lawyer says things are going in the right direction. He thinks that ultimately he'll be able to get her out and keep her from being deported." Taking the opening, Clare said, "Actually, right now I'm down near Immokalee hoping to help finish up one of the unanswered questions we need if we're going to get her out."

"Immokalee? Isn't that a long way from Sarasota? Are you driving back tonight?"

"No, we're not going back yet."

"We're not going back? What's going on Clare? This sounds strange to me."

"Well – it's a little strange, but it's what I need to do." Her voice caught a little, which she didn't want to happen. But it seemed harder to hide her fear from Kate than from herself.

"Clare are you okay? Who is we?" She demanded.

"We is Paul and me, and yes I'm okay. I'm just tired. I've really got to go now." Before she asked for any more details.

"Well – whatever is going on, I guess it's good you're not alone. Call me tomorrow okay?"

"Love you."

"Love you too."

Staring at the wall - Clare admitted to herself that she was afraid. Still driven - still sure that she wanted to see this through - but inside she felt herself shaking. Whatever was happening in this town, she could feel in her bones something was very wrong.

Clare closed her eyes - without much hope of sleep. She tried to slow her breathing, tried to picture the church service with the candles and the music. She remembered a line from Sunday School - "Be still and know that I am God." She breathed in the stillness and let the words meet all her worries. A calmness came upon her, as she heard the words 'Choose Peace.' Choose Peace - she did her best to plant those words in her soul - hoping they'd be with her for whatever the next day would bring.

# Chapter 45

The first call they got from Gus told them to go to a restaurant around the corner from the Coalition. They ordered the special of the day, had a delicious meal, and Gus never showed up. Then, Paul got a text, telling them to meet him at the slavery museum, which turned out to be in a box truck that police had rescued slaves from. The slaves had paid a whole lot of money to people who had told them they could get them documents to work in the U.S. Then they got to the U.S., and the crew bosses refused to give them any papers, or even pay them for the work they made them do. At night the workers had been padlocked in, chained up with no windows, no light, no fresh air, after working all day in the fields. Finally, they made it out by digging a hole by hand into the top of the truck, big enough for one of the men to get out and run for help. It was a deeply disturbing story – unbelievable to Clare that they were talking about something that had happened this close to home, in this century.

It was a good idea for a place to meet though. They didn't stick out so much there as they did on the streets of the town. This time Gus did come. He stood nearby as if he was looking at the same exhibit they were looking at.

"I'm almost positive that there's a rescue attempt in progress. If I'm right they are going to take whoever they find to the hospital – no matter what shape they appear to be in. I need you to get me from here to the hospital, so I can determine if Roberto is one of the rescued, or if not, whether they've ever seen him. I need to be at the hospital when they bring in whoever they find, so I can try to talk to them before they shut down communication."

"What hospital are we talking about?"

"They didn't say that – I'm lucky I got this much. The waitress at the restaurant seems to be part of the undercover operation. I ate there everyday since I got here, because I got the sense it was a more important place than it was supposed to be. Sure enough, I watched her get a note from somebody one day. When I showed her a picture that I got from Maria's lawyer, and told her how important this was to this man's wife and children, she knew I knew something. She told me to keep out of the way – but that I might have my answers very soon."

Clare got out her phone and started looking for hospitals.

"I don't think they'll take them to the nearest hospital. There's too much in this town that doesn't feel right – I don't think they'd chance something happening to whoever they are able to get out."

"Okay – so there's a hospital in Naples. Do you think they'd go that far?"

"Yeah – unless somebody's dying – they'd go that far."

"Naples Memorial. It's about 25 miles from here. We need to just take Immokalee Rd. cross over the highway and follow the Blue Hospital signs. Do you want to leave now?"

"Yes," Gus said, looking around and seeing no one watching. "Right now." Gus followed them to the car, and slid into the backseat without looking back at the town he'd spent the last few days in. She wondered where he'd slept, then realized that for Gus this wasn't an issue. Whether he slept on the street or in one of the shelters, he'd know how to adjust. Clare on the other hand –between the strange location, the nervousness about what today would bring, and the arguments she'd had with Paul - she'd hardly slept at all.

"Gus, What if it's not Roberto?" She asked the question, almost wishing she hadn't as soon as the words were out of her mouth. Because she knew there was no good answer.

"If it's not Roberto – it could still be someone who knows him or knew him. I'll still keep looking for him. But truthfully, if it's not Roberto – I'm not sure we'll have the answer Maria's attorney needs in time to do her any good. He'll just have to hope there's nothing somebody else found that causes her more trouble."

"Do you think that could happen?"

"Could happen – sure anything's possible. But, I'm pretty good at finding things, and I didn't find it." Clare smiled at this confident Gus that she hadn't really seen before. "Plus, I don't think it will happen."

"Because?"

"Because I think if they get somebody out today – it's going to be Roberto."

Clare fell silent, wanting to stay in the hopeful picture Gus was painting for her.

Paul seemed to be concentrating on the driving much more than he did on the way down. He kept looking at the fields on the sides of the roads, as if he expected there to be a turn ahead, but they already knew there were no turns for miles and miles. Clare wondered what was on his mind. Finally, he spoke. "Gus, all these orange groves, do you think there are slaves in all these fields?"

"Well, I'm not an expert, I've only got a few days more perspective than the two of you, but no, I don't think so. I think the slavery is the worst of the issues down here, but it's not like everyone you see is a slave. There are lots of problems though even if you aren't a slave. Lots of abuse from what I could see at the shelter. On the other hand – across from the parking lot where people get picked up to work in the fields is where the Coalition has offices– and people really seem to think that place has their back. Somebody came to town for the first time when I was there, and people were telling them to go over there and check it out."

As they got closer to Naples, Clare started to question Gus' plan. They might accept Gus as a person who had a right to ask any questions he wanted, but to the world, Gus still looked the guy with the sweater he never took off, holes in his shoes, and rips in his pants. Any hospital security guard would likely stop him. Clare didn't want to hurt Gus' feelings, but this seemed too important not to say.

"Gus, I'm afraid that you might not get by without attracting attention in a Naples hospital. That's a pretty rich area."

"Yeah – which doesn't mean there aren't homeless people there, but I do see your point. I need something different to wear. If you see a Salvation Army shop – stop real quick okay Paul?"

"We're in a hurry though. How about I just lend you my clothes? I think they'd fit you." Paul said.

Gus shook his head, laughing. "Then you'd have to wear my clothes or drive around in your underwear – which I'm pretty sure is illegal."

"Well, do you mind if I wear your clothes?"

"No – I guess it wouldn't be that bad for you – those people at the shelter just washed them." Paul was already pulling into a gas station parking lot, before Gus had time to change his mind. It made her smile that Paul would think of this option. Wearing somebody else's clothes, that was pretty intimate. Whatever boundaries any of them had thought they had seemed to go out the window compared to trying to find Roberto for Maria.

It struck her when they came out switched that they could have had each other's life. Crazy that the clothes mattered that much. But like it or not, the new Gus had a much better chance of getting in to see Roberto.

"Where do you want us to take you?"

"Drop me at the E.R. My guess is that they'll be busy enough that if I come in complaining of something small, I'll be able to hang around as long as I need to, without attracting attention. That way when they bring in whoever they're bringing in – I'll already be there, and hopefully I'll be able to confirm that we have Roberto back."

"What if you're wrong about all this – the whole hospital thing, even which hospital – there's a lot of guess work here. I don't know…."

"Clare, I have pretty good intuition. That's what I have to go on. It's not always right, but it is right more often than not. You don't have to believe me, but I think you'll feel better if you do." His confidence was noticeable again. Somehow, Clare had the sense she was speaking to the Gus of ten or even twenty years ago.

"Okay Gus. I'll go with trusting you. What do Paul and I do after we drop you off?"

"You go home."

"What?"  Paul didn't like that answer at all. "Look, Gus, we want to help. We're willing to stay around, and take you back when you're ready, or bail you out if this mess gets you into some kind of trouble."

Gus looked at both of them, as if deciding what he should say.

"Look guys – you've been really helpful already. But now, I really need you to go, so that I'm not worrying about you. My sense is that once they have Roberto in the hospital he'll be safe, but I don't know that – and I don't want to be distracted."

Paul tried appealing to the Gus they knew back home. "But what about your clothes?  How will I get them back to you?" Typically, Gus would have wanted his clothes back as soon as possible.

"Don't worry. I'll find you back at Manna House. Probably by tomorrow night. I think I can trust you until then." He smiled at Paul, as if he were indulging a child, who'd tried a trick that didn't have a chance of working.

As they approached the large Naples hospital, Gus' face changed. Right in front of Clare's eyes, he became someone else. Strong, smart, handsome even, in an older man kind of way. Whatever Gus' story was, whatever his past life had been, it was clear to Clare that he had gone back to it, to do what Maria needed done.

They slowed down near the entry to the E.R., and Gus jumped out of the car. "Goodbye," he said. "And thanks. I'll be in touch. Go home now. Please." He looked at Paul as he said that.

"We will Gus. We will."

As they drove away, Clare said, "Somehow I'm getting a good feeling. I think it's going to be Roberto. I think it's going to be okay."

Paul nodded. "I hope so. I hope it is Roberto. And I hope he's okay. I guess that's all we can do now. Hope." His voice sounded more hopeless than hopeful.

"Look Paul – I think that's the only option we've got – except for praying – and I think we might want to take that option too."

"You're right. I know you're right." He became quiet, and Clare had the sense that they were both silently praying for Gus, for Roberto, for whoever else might be trapped in this modern-day slavery Clare hadn't known existed a week ago.

# Chapter 46

When Paul dropped her at her house, she was so tired she wanted to just jump into bed, even though it was only eight o'clock, but then she saw that she had messages, and made herself listen.

It was Pete, telling her that if she didn't get into the office tomorrow, she didn't have a chance of keeping her job. He actually kind of sounded sad about that, which was nice of him. Clare was so exhausted, that even the thought of a confrontation with the partners didn't wreck her sleep.

But it did wake her up early. She woke before the alarm and began considering what she would and wouldn't tell them about how she'd spent the last few days. If they seemed like they'd listen to her, she might just tell them the truth, and see what they'd do with that. But if they were doing all the talking and didn't want to hear reason... she wasn't sure what she'd do.

Clare got in early. She went directly to Pete's office, where she found him staring into space. He seemed startled to see her.

"You're here."

"I'm here."

"Did you decide your job was worth saving?"

"I finished what I needed to do, so I came home."

"Jack is the partner you need to talk to now. He wanted me to tell him when and if you got here. He wants to see you." Pete got up and motioned her to follow him. "I'm going to stay with you in case he wants me to give you a reference as to your work quality prior to this infraction."

"Infraction?"

"Yes, infraction."

"So, out of curiosity, what will you say about my work quality prior to the "infraction?"

"I'll tell them you are the best junior I've worked with since I've been here."

"Wow. Thanks." It was good to hear him say that out loud.

"It's true."

They walked into the office, which she'd only seen from the hallway. Mahogany bookcases, a captain's desk, sculpture on the shelves. Gorgeous, but totally intimidating. Jack's office walls had lots of pictures. Pictures of his family - four children of varying ages. And other pictures of him shaking hands with important people, like the Governor of Florida.

"Jack, you remember Clare Wheeler?  She came in bright and early this morning."  Pete's attempt to speak for her was starting right from the beginning.

"Ms. Wheeler, it is my understanding that you haven't been here this week. Is that correct?" Jack Anderson didn't waste any time.

"Yes sir."

"It is also my understanding that you were informed that you are not allowed time off during the period between February 15th and April 15th according to the contract you signed when you began employment here. Is that correct?"

"Yes sir."

"Your Senior Accountant has been trying to tell us you are worth a second chance. But bluntly, we don't do that, because if we did, then our clause would be meaningless, and we can't run this firm without staff during those two months."

Clare realized that this might really be it. She thought she'd known that all along, but the rock that had suddenly appeared in the pit of her stomach told her otherwise.

"Do you have anything you want to say to me Ms. Wheeler?"

"Well, I want to say I'm sorry I let you down."

Pete spoke up. "Clare, I think you should tell him why you were out. For that matter, I'd like to know more too. Tell us why this was so important to you."

"Will it make a difference?"  Clare asked.

"Probably not." Jack Anderson was clearly not a person to pretend anything that wasn't true, that was for sure.

Pete looked at her. "Tell him. They need to know you weren't just off partying at the beach."  Pete looked at Jack, and she realized there was anger running under the surface of Pete's polite face.

"Well, a friend of mine was in trouble." Clare started.

"What kind of trouble?" Jack interrupted.

The truth and nothing but the truth, she decided. Otherwise, what was the point of saying anything at all? "Well, the underlying issue was immigration trouble. I have a friend who was pulled over for driving someone else's car that had a broken taillight. But, since she was undocumented, the problem got very serious, very fast. Her kids were born here, and I felt like I needed to do everything I could to help them be raised by their mother, not by strangers."

"So, you were taking care of this woman's children?" Pete asked.

"No, I was in Immokalee, trying to get information that would help her stay in this country. I know it's complicated, but it was something I had to do, to help her, and to help another friend of mine who was in danger because he'd been working on getting information to help her too."

Jack had listened to what she'd said, and clearly had something to say himself. "Ms. Wheeler, I don't think you have the proper respect for the law to work at our firm. I have to say I don't agree with your decision to try to help an illegal person stay in this country."

Clare felt her blood pressure rise. Wasn't this the man who had tried to convince her to 'make the numbers say the right thing?' He had the gall to call her not respectful enough of the law? Still she kept her voice as calm as she could. "She's not an illegal person. She's a person whose husband helped pick the tomatoes you eat on your salad. She's a mother to two awesome children. Not having the right papers doesn't make you an illegal person. It just means you don't have the right papers."

"It means she came here illegally."

"Maybe - I don't know exactly how she got here. But I do know the illegal part you are so concerned about doesn't tell you anything about who she is. And the job she's done over the years isn't one that she took out of an American citizen's hands - no one was lining up to do the work she's been doing."

"Illegal is illegal! There's no room to talk about anything else." Jack Anderson's eyes were flashing right back at her.

Clare looked over at Pete, who clearly didn't know what to say. She couldn't read his face, couldn't tell who he agreed with, if he had an opinion at all.

"Look Mr. Anderson, I'll make this easy on you. You don't have to fire me, and you won't have to worry about me collecting unemployment. I'll just resign. I can see that this is not a place I want to work anymore." The words came easily to her tongue.

Pete protested. "Clare, no. Don't do that."

Mr. Anderson shook his head. "She's right Pete. She needs to leave. For all kinds of reasons." The conversation was over, and he was already moving back to his desk to start the rest of the day.

They walked out of the office, and Clare could hardly believe that she'd been able to say everything she'd said. She was shaken from the experience of standing up to this powerful man the way she had - but at the same time, she was proud that she'd had that in her. And about deciding to quit - she was totally at peace. She didn't want to work for this firm anymore. Bluntly, she didn't want to make one more penny for that man.

"Pete, thank you for what you said in there. I really appreciated it."

"You know, I think he might have let you stay. We really need you to get through the busy season."

"I'm sorry about that Pete. I know you'll probably end up having to put in even more overtime, and I feel bad about that. I really do. But after hearing what he said today, this just isn't a place I want to work anymore. This just isn't a place I can imagine working for one more minute."

"Well, I admire your passion, if not your common sense. And I'll give you a reference. Hopefully, it won't affect you when you try to get a new job that you quit during busy season." He looked concerned, and he was right. That could look bad to a potential future employer. Well, one step at a time. Right now, she just needed to clean out her desk, and get out of there.

# Chapter 47

She didn't take much time, just quickly put things in a box and was out of the main office area before people even came in for the morning. Looking around the office as she left, she felt a little sorrow about the people she wouldn't see at work anymore. And she also felt a little relief that she'd been good about putting money in her savings account - so she wasn't going to be broke for at least a little while. She walked as quickly as she could to her car, not looking in either direction, not wanting to have to explain where she was going to any of her early arriving co-workers. That's why she didn't see him, until he was almost directly in front of her.

"Clare?"

The voice didn't do what it used to do at all. Instead - she felt her heart sink.

"Danny." He stood between her and her car.

"I texted you and you didn't answer."

"Yeah - well that's what happens when you break up with people. They don't answer your texts." She heard the emotion in her voice and was aware that it didn't really all belong to Danny. "What is it?"

"Can we talk?"

She almost said, 'Go ahead - say whatever you need to say.' But then she realized she didn't want anyone witnessing this conversation. She was about to be the subject of too much talk already, as people tried to figure out what happened to her, and why she was gone. She didn't want to add to the gossip, by having a fight with her ex in the parking lot on her way off the property for the last time.

"Okay. I need to drop these things in my car. Then you can follow me to a coffee shop, over by the mall." Danny looked relieved that she was willing to talk with him, without any more pleading. He didn't even seem to notice that she had a box with a desk full of stuff in her arms.

She drove to the coffee shop on automatic pilot. Her brain felt totally overwhelmed, with the reality of leaving her job, and Danny showing up yet again - for who knows what reason.

She didn't even wait for him to get out of his car, just went into the coffee shop, ordered a latte and found a table, leaving him to order for himself, as if he wasn't even with her.

When he sat down, she said, "Okay - what are you doing here?"

"Well - it's not because the band got a job or anything like that. I just got on a plane yesterday afternoon and came directly to Sarasota, and I've been trying to find you."

"How did you find me?"   It hadn't even occurred to her to wonder that at first.

"I found minutes of a board meeting online that had your name in it. A symphony. They mentioned you and the firm you work for, and I looked up the firm, and decided I would just watch and see if you came in. But you must have gotten there really early, because when I saw you, you were coming out."

"Well - that was pretty good detective work. But why did you do it?"

"It's… It's…well…" He was stuck. She almost felt sorry for him.

"Just say it Danny."   She wondered what it could be this time. Their last meeting had been so bad - but it had given her the closure she needed. Maybe he needed a different kind of closure?

He looked up, directly into her eyes. "I don't know how to say this, but to just say it. I'm supposed to be getting married next week, and all I can think about is you. Your smile. Your laugh. The way you always knew the right thing to say. I miss you Clare. I think I want you." He moved closer to her and began to take her hand.

Clare took a deep breath. There was a time when she would have imagined there would never be such a thing as too late, when it came to Danny.

She pulled her hand away - gently. "Danny - I loved you. I mean, I really loved you. I thought it was for forever. But, in the last year, I've changed, in ways I never could have imagined. For example, today I quit my job, without another one waiting for me."

Danny's eyes registered surprise.

"I know. You didn't realize. You didn't ask me what I was doing leaving work or carrying all my personal stuff in a box. You weren't thinking about me at all. You were thinking about you, and what you wanted and that's just not enough for me anymore. I need to live my life, not just be the supporting player in yours."

He started to object to that - but Clare put up her hand.

"I'm not saying that's your fault. That's just the relationship we made. And now, I want something more." He looked miserable.

"Danny - are you sure you're not just getting scared? Wanting to go backwards to the way life used to be, instead of doing grown-up things like working and getting married?"

"I don't think so. I think I really miss you."

"But what about Michelle? I thought you really seemed to love her, and even admire her, when we talked before."

"We had a fight. A big one."

"Is the wedding off?"

"No - but it might be when she finds out I came down here."

"You're right. It might. Do you want it to be?" Clare asked.

"I don't know. Maybe not. Maybe you're right that I'm just scared and I'm freaking out. I don't know."

"So - go talk to her. See what's going on in her head. Give the two of you a chance." Clare couldn't believe how calmly she could give Danny advice. If she'd wondered even for a second if she was over him - that thought was put to rest for good.

"So - I'm leaving now. Thank you for coming to see me - and thank you for telling me you missed me. It was kind of nice to hear." She meant that. There was something reassuring about knowing that their relationship had left some kind of a mark on him too. But now - it was really, really over.

"Good luck Clare - finding your next job, I mean. Whatever it turns out to be, I hope you love it."

She paused at his words. Was there something out there she could love, like he loved music? She hoped so - she really hoped so.

"Thanks Danny, I hope so too. Good luck to you - and goodbye."

# Chapter 48

Her first decision as an unemployed woman was to go home, get a book, and enter into somebody else's world for a while. Hers had become overwhelming.

She was picking a book from her shelf to reread, when the phone rang, and Clare automatically answered.

"Hi Clare, it's Paul. I know this is a long shot. I was just wondering if you might be able to get free for a few minutes this afternoon?"

Clare didn't say that as of this morning, she was pretty much free anytime. She just said, "Yes."

"Would you like to come with me to Maria's lawyer? He called and said he wanted to meet with us at two."

"Definitely! I'm glad you got me. I really want to hear what he has to say first hand."

She hung up the phone - then decided that she needed to tell her family what had happened. She decided to call and leave messages - knowing her parents would be at work, and Kate would hopefully be at class. That way she'd be able to control her emotions and help them feel like she was okay.

"Hey it's me. Just wanted you to know I decided to leave my job today. I realized the values of the firm weren't a good fit for me. Don't worry. I'm really okay."

Clare knew they'd worry anyway, and Kate would be mad she hadn't discussed this with her before doing it. But the voice in her head had become strong enough now that she trusted it. She liked living this way - trusting herself to be who she was, no matter what.

Driving up to the attorney's office, she saw Paul waiting for her.

She parked and got out saying, "Did he give you any hint? Is it good news?"

"I hope so." Paul looked more nervous than she felt. She wondered why, but she didn't have time to ask before he opened the door and gave their names to the secretary.

As soon as they walked in the office, Clare felt the good news vibrating through their lawyer. "I'm glad you could both be here. So, we've got some really good news. And I gotta say, I don't get to say those words as often as I'd like."

She felt her face ease into a smile. "Well, don't keep us guessing. What's the good news?"

"First, the private eye found Maria's husband. And there were no charges outstanding against him, nothing to make our case weaker. So, with that information, I went to the D.A. We got lucky. We drew Winston, and he hates breaking up families. Once I told him that Maria and her family were totally clean, and made the case that the kids were citizens, and Maria would probably leave them here, he knew they would be better off with her than any foster family we'd be able to come up with – so - he agreed to let her go. He's not even making her pay the ticket for the broken tail light, since the car didn't belong to her any way."

"So, she's free?" It seemed impossible, but Clare wasn't going to argue.

"She's free as of tomorrow. She'll make a court appearance, and everything will get waived."

"What about her husband?"

"That's the part of the story that's really unbelievable. My private eye found out that her husband had answered an ad for workers at double the usual rate and ended up in a forced labor situation. He couldn't leave or contact anybody, because the crew boss threatened to turn him and Maria over to the authorities. Plus, they kept promising that they were holding big sums of money for him. Even showed him bank account statements. He knew it probably wasn't true, but he didn't feel like he had any choice but to keep working for them. The authorities had been looking for a way to break this from the inside, so they could not only get people out, but bring down the crew bosses whole operation. My guy got connected locally, and apparently got him a message that Maria was in trouble. So, this Roberto volunteered to be the first one to try the new version of the underground railroad they were building, and he made it out. He didn't leave with the money he'd supposedly earned, but he got his life back."

"So, are you telling us Maria's husband is on his way back home?" The rollercoaster Maria had been on was about to take a turn that sounded miraculous.

"He's home. He's going to find an apartment, and they'll have a place to live once Maria and the kids get released."

"An apartment?  I thought you said he left without his money."

"Yeah – I'm not sure where he got the first month's rent and security deposit."

Clare turned and looked at Paul, but he shook his head. "Not that I wouldn't have been willing to help, but I'm hearing the story for the first time, same as you."

And then she knew. Gus. Somehow Gus had to have given Roberto the money, so that he and Maria could have a home to start over in. Gus, who would probably sleep on the street tonight, would give everything he had to help somebody else.

"Thank you."  She was overwhelmed with the success this man had had, in a situation that had seemed hopeless. "Really, thank you."

His face actually turned a little red. "It's okay. I'm glad I could help this lady. She's a good lady."

"Yes, she is. And a good Mom too."

He smiled again, then glanced at all the papers on his desk. Clare felt like she could almost see the brain moving behind his eyes. He needed them to go, so that he could move on to the next person, the next file. Clare wondered who was next, what their story was. She said a silent prayer as they left that whoever it was would have as good of an outcome as Maria had had.

Paul had a smile on his face, one she hadn't seen in a while. "I've gotta tell you, when we started this whole thing, I thought the outcome was going to be horrible. I've been trying to figure out if Maria had any relatives, so that someone could come and be with the kids if they deported her."

She looked at him quizzically. "Did you find anybody?"

"No. No one. Dead ends all over the place. Good thing being a private detective isn't my real job."

"Which reminds me – are you thinking what I'm thinking?"

"You mean about Gus?  Yeah, I think he must have used the money he got for expenses to set Roberto and Maria and the kids up in an apartment. Do you think that's why he's homeless? Cuz he gives all his money away?"

"I don't know. I've never asked him – Manna House rules you know." Clare laughed. The thing was though, Gus no longer felt like a Manna House guest. He was a person she could imagine trusting if she needed help, a person who could function quite well in the world, a person she'd seen working, first-hand. Maybe the Manna House rules didn't apply in this situation anymore. And then she started thinking about all the rules that seemed to be up in the air in her life at the moment.

Clare heard herself say it out loud for the first time. "I left my job today. They were really angry that I wasn't in the last few days, and when I tried to explain, the things the partner said made me so angry, I just couldn't work there anymore."

Paul looked at her, waiting to see if there was anything else she wanted to say, but there wasn't. She had let herself say that her job was finished, and when she did, she knew it was true. What she didn't know is what the next sentence would be.

Finally, Paul spoke. "It hurts, doesn't it?"

"Yeah – it does." And then she remembered that he knew what it felt like to know your job was done, what it felt like to realize you needed to move on.

"Do you have savings to get you through?"

"A little. Not as much as I wish I had, but enough to get me through a few months."

"Do you think they'll give you a good reference, so you can find something else?"

"Yeah – my supervisor Pete will. He was really a decent guy. He tried to get them to listen to me, and he told them I was good at my job. And even after I resigned, which really put him in a bad position, he still said he'd give me a good reference."

"Can you ask your parents to help you?'

"I guess I could. They're paying for part of Kate's school already – so I'm not sure how much they'd be able to do."

"Well, if you have a little put away, give yourself some time to grieve before you jump into the job search. Otherwise, your first interviews will come out sounding hollow."

"Spoken like someone who knows?"

"Yeah. I realized no one tells you that leaving a job is going to be hard, that you'll miss the people you shared your days with. Even when you leave for something really terrific, there's grief there. And when you leave for empty air – it's that much worse."

"Thanks for giving me something else to look forward to," Clare smiled as she said the words.

"I do that to you a lot don't I. I'm like the bad news bringer in your life." He wasn't smiling. He looked really sad.

"It's okay."

"It's not actually. Because I don't want to be that guy. I want to be the guy who comforts you, the guy you love to talk to, the name on the caller id you can't wait to answer."

And Clare turned, and she looked into his eyes, and she saw a mixture of pain and tenderness that took her breath away.

"I know – too much. Too much for you right now. Maybe too much for you ever."

"No. No. Not too much. Just – I need to get through some things in the next few days. And…" And she didn't know what to say next. And she didn't want to confuse her neediness right at this moment for something else. And she couldn't handle losing Paul as a friend if they tried a relationship and it didn't work. And…

"And, my timing stinks." Now he was smiling, letting her off the hook, being the one to say no. She was relieved – kind of.

"One day at a time. That's what you need right now. To go one day at a time, through the craziness of leaving your job, through the waking up in the morning with no where to go."

"That won't be good?  Like vacation?"

"Nothing like vacation. But you will have one option that I didn't have."

"Which is?"

"Manna House. You can come in as much or as little as you want. You'll always know there are people there who want to see you."

Clare felt a sense of peace where only a moment before there'd been nothing but nerves. Paul was right. There was a rock in her life. A solid place. Not her job, which is what she'd always assumed. It was Manna House that would remain, while everything else might change.

# Chapter 49

Clare woke up the first day of the next chapter of her life, and feeling the emptiness Paul had predicted, got herself up and out to the beach. And the beach did its part to heal her. The sun was just right, the ocean the beautiful blue green color that she didn't take for granted, having come from a childhood of ponds and lakes, without waves or color to make them interesting. She watched the water, and breathed in and out, until finally, she allowed her thoughts to rest on the challenge that had suddenly come her way.

And then, just like that Gus was standing in front of her. Not in her imagination, but the real person, close enough to touch. She looked around, to make sure she wasn't messing up some surveillance he had in place, then quietly said, "Gus?"

He turned, and with what felt to her like a gigantic sigh of relief, he came to her and put out his arms, to give her a hug.

"You're back!" He looked good, and he felt stronger than usual as she hugged him.

"I'm back."

"And you're okay?"

"Yes, I'm okay.

"Paul and I met with the attorney yesterday for Maria, and it sounds like everything is almost all worked out."

"Yes – I think they are going to be fine."

"Gus, I'm just going to say it. I know you're helping Roberto and Maria. You really are amazing."

"Look, I'm happy I got to do it, I'm happy I found him, I wish I would have looked before. I don't know why it took her getting in trouble." Unbelievable. The guy was a hero in this situation, and he couldn't even see it, because he was too busy wishing he'd done something earlier.

"Gus, so help me, if you turn this around to make it as if you didn't do the right thing, when you're just about the only person I know who always seems to try to do the right thing – I'll..."

"You'll what?" Now he was laughing at her inability to complete a sentence.

"I don't know. I'll keep telling you what a great guy you are, I guess. Maybe someday you'll believe it."

"Thanks – thanks Clare. Really."

"Gus, can I ask you something?  You don't have to answer."

"Okay – go ahead."

"I mean you really don't have to answer."  Now she was starting to chicken out, just as she had the door to her curiosity almost opened.

"What is it?"

"Gus, in the last week, it's become pretty obvious you are perfectly capable of being an awesome investigator. And so, I'm just wondering, if you can do this kind of work so well, why are you on the streets?"  It was out, and her nerves were even worse than they'd been her first night at Manna House. She didn't want to scare him off; she didn't want him to go underground, which it occurred to her only at that moment, he could do better than most people.

"Well, it's a fair question. If you'd asked me before I wouldn't have been ready to talk about it. But now – I'll try."  He stopped, and she didn't say a word, or move a muscle. If he was ready to talk, all she wanted to do was listen.

"I haven't been doing this kind of work for a long time. I mean I used to. I used to do this work full-time – had clients with offices in high rises that had a view of the ocean. Picked and chose too. No messy divorce work, just the kind of work that made sense to me. Finding missing people. Uncovering fraud, or embezzlers. That kind of work. I liked it, actually. I was one of the few people I knew who got up in the morning and liked what I did. From the time I was a kid, I liked solving mysteries I guess. So, when I stopped writing for that paper I told you about, I began to get the stories behind the scenes."

He paused, and she could see he had gone back in time. Finally, he went on. "It was all good, until the day this man, name was Frank. Frank Richards. He called me to his office, and he told me he needed me to find his daughter. He said she'd gotten mixed up with some bad people, and he wasn't mad at her – but he wanted her home. He wanted her safe. And so, I looked for his daughter. Her name was Eve, and she was 18, and I finally found her up in Gainesville. She wasn't going to school up there; she was just sleeping on people's couches. And I talked to her, and she told me her Dad was evil. She said he used to beat her, and torment her and as soon as she could, she had taken off, and she begged me not to tell him where she was."   Gus' eyes were tearing up, and Clare wanted to tell him he could stop talking. But she stayed silent.

"I didn't believe her. I thought her father was telling me the truth. I thought she was into drugs, that she was with a bad group of college kids. His story made sense to me, and hers didn't. I mean, she wasn't doing anything but sleeping on people's couches. Like I told you, I've always had good intuition, but back then I went too far with it. Prided myself on believing people couldn't lie to me. So, I told her I was sorry, but I had to tell her father where she was. And she ran out of the room, and she locked herself in the bathroom, and by the time I got the door open — there was blood everywhere. I called 911, but she was dead by the time the ambulance arrived."

He stopped, and she could see in his eyes that the pain hadn't lessened over the years. Then he said, "When her Dad got there, I wanted to believe that I'd been right. That what she'd done, she'd done because she was high, and bad as it was, I'd just pushed her over the edge she'd have fallen from eventually. But there was something different about that man when he got there. He was sad, moaning sad, but his eyes were hard and full of tears at the same time. I'd never seen that before, or since actually. Then he looked for her stuff, and when he found her journal, he took out a match and lit it on fire. And I knew that whatever had been in there, whatever stories she'd told about him, I knew they were true."

"When I left her apartment, I couldn't go home. I couldn't go anywhere. I never did. Never did go home, never did go back to my office. I wanted to disappear, but I couldn't make it happen the way she did. It was like I owed it to Eve to be in pain."

He stopped, and she didn't say anything. Clare knew trying to tell him it was okay, or any other comforting cliché would be an affront to the story he'd told her.

Finally, she broke the silence. "And now?  Do you still feel you owe her your life?"

"Yes, but lately I've been feeling like I owe her my life in a different way. Like I owe it to her to be on the other side."

"What does that mean?"

"I owe it to her to be on the side of people like her. The people running. The people who can't pay for the help they need. Those people need what I can do way more than the people I used to work for."

"So, what does that mean for you?"

"What do you mean?" Gus asked.

"Will you open a business for those people, move into an apartment again?"

"No. Why would I do that? The people I want to help, they live on the street, and they know me as one of them. I don't want money from them. I want to help my friends – any of them I can." There was something in his voice – hope maybe. Purpose maybe. Maybe a little of both.

"Gus, where did you get the money to help Maria and Roberto? It doesn't seem like the expense money would have been enough to set them up, even if you didn't use any of it for your trip."

"There's this guy. He lives in my old place. He found me – I guess he's kind of an amateur detective himself, and he wanted my old apartment. I'd paid cash for it, and I guess the bank account I had before Eve had enough in it, that the automatic payments I set up paid my taxes, and all the condo bills. He owned the one next to it, and he wanted to cut through to mine, because he was marrying someone with a family, and so the association told him they couldn't find me. So, he looked for me, and he found me, and I told him just take it, just make it into your family's home. But he wouldn't do that. Every month he finds me, and he gives me a check. I guess his wife thinks he's crazy to do that, so he pays it out of his work, but he says he couldn't live there in peace if he thought of me on the street every time he walks in. When he gives me the check, he feels like he's giving me a choice, and that - he can live with. So, I take it, and I put it in the bank – figured that was the right thing to do for the guy, you know? Turned out to be a good thing, I guess because that's where the extra money for Maria's family came from.

"One more question. Do you have a family? People who might be looking for you."

"I have a family, but they aren't looking for me. They know where I am."

"And they're okay with it?"

"Clare – my family are the people at Manna House. They are the only people who look for me when I'm gone and call 911 when I fall down in the street. They're my family, and I'm their family." It wasn't the answer to the question she'd been asking, but she knew he was right.

Clare put her hand on Gus' shoulder, and he didn't pull away. She turned her face so that he could see directly into her eyes and she said, "Gus, all the good you've done since that terrible night, all the good you're going to do, it means that girl's life made a difference. She died, and that hurts more than I can imagine, I know that. But I hope someday you can find some peace in knowing that she still lives in you. You've made sure her life counted."

Gus looked down at the ground. She could see the tears in his eyes, though he didn't want her to. "Thanks Clare. Thanks for caring about me. I mean, you always do."

"I always will." Whatever came next in her life, Clare suddenly knew she wouldn't be moving. Manna House was part of her too now. The world might define her by her profession, or lack thereof, but she could decide to define herself by what she loved, and what she loved was serving the people at Manna House.

# Chapter 50

The sun had to really shine to get her attention the next morning. Done with her job, Clare saw no more reason to set an alarm. Nothing wrong with sleeping in rather than early morning resume writing. When she finally got up, the red light on her phone was flashing that there were messages. Paul, just checking on her. Kate, just checking on her. Her parents, just checking on her. Clare went on the computer, and played with her resume until noon, then called and left messages when she knew her friends and family would be busy. She didn't want to talk. She just wanted to be alone in her world, to let the reality sink in. The reality that she was alone. The reality that she didn't have a place to go every morning. She got out pen and paper and tried to write out how she felt. She wanted to let it out, and let herself move on, but after about six pages, she could tell it wasn't going to come out as easily as she wanted it to.

After some days, Clare felt ready to start answering the phone again, so when Kate's number popped up, she picked up the line. "Clare – you gotta get up and get started looking. I'm sorry, but this time Mom and Dad are right." Kate's nagging voice wasn't what she'd expected. Support, maybe a little push, but not nagging.

"I know. I really do know. It's just that I'm having a hard time figuring out what I'm looking for."

"Well, you've been leaving me that message for two weeks, and you don't seem to be any closer to knowing. Have you ever thought that maybe if you start applying you'll begin to figure it out?"

"Two weeks doesn't seem like that long to me."

"How much savings do you have?"

"Okay – maybe two weeks is long enough. Today I'll finish my resume. I'll leave off the objective line at the top, and hope something comes to me later."

"Either that, or just write my objective is to get a job doing whatever job you are applying for."

"That's so – I don't know – fake..."

"Whatever – just do it. It's time sister. You gotta get up off the mat."

Clare could tell she was worried. Her family had obviously decided she felt like she got fired, which would have most likely been true if she hadn't quit. They were worried that she was getting depressed.

But the truth was, depression wasn't what she was feeling at all. What she was feeling – was free. What she was feeling – was that a weight had been taken off her, and now she just had to figure out what weight she wanted to pick up in its place. The one that would fit her.

Clare wondered if Kate was right, that applying for things would help her figure out what she did or didn't want to do. It was worth a try, so she got the resume done and started surfing through the opportunities in the local paper. Since it was busy season, there were quite a few. Nothing that stood out though.

It was Sunday, and it hit her that it might be good to get out into the world again – so she got herself ready for the evening service over at the church. Maybe the quiet would give her some sense of possibility. Maybe praying was what she needed to be doing more of.

The service was just beginning when she went in, and she slipped into the pew, seeing that the candles were set in the front tonight. The piano music was so peaceful. She didn't know the name of the songs – but they were just right for her mood. Closing her eyes, the notes pulled her in, until she wasn't thinking anymore, she was finally just breathing.

When the service ended, she stayed put. And then Susan, from Shepherd's Center, who she hadn't even noticed before, came over to her.

"Do you have a minute? Can we talk?" Susan asked.

They went out to the hallway, and Susan said, "I called over to your firm, and they said you weren't there anymore."

"Yes, we had a parting of the ways."

"I'm sorry. I mean I'm really sorry. You helped me so much."

"Thanks. It was really great working with you."

"So, I was wondering if you are interested in some work?"

"Oh, I can't work on any of my former clients. I signed an agreement about that when I joined the firm."

"Of course. No, this is something else. One of my friends runs a non-profit mission small business, where she sends first aid kits overseas, and she was telling me her books were kind of a mess. What if I give her your number?"

The yes was out of her mouth so fast, she couldn't believe it. She gave Susan all her numbers, and instructions to tell her friend to call anytime.

Driving home, she felt more excited than she'd felt in a long time. Maybe this was it, her new career. Maybe there was a whole segment of people who were trying to do good things who had no clue how to do their books so that they could keep the I.R.S. and their donors happy. Maybe she could help those people fix their accounting messes.

After living with the idea for a few hours, she decided that it had long-term potential. The question was, how would she pay the bills while she was building this business up? Her reserves wouldn't last long enough to do that.

Clare kept looking at the papers, but there was nothing listed that felt as right as her idea. By Thursday, she was ready for something to distract her from her job situation. She'd gone to Manna House the week before, and it had really filled the void. It had been so good to see Velma and Gus, Maria and her kids. And she got to meet Roberto, who seemed exactly like the kind of guy Maria should be with. It felt like a reunion, and their hugs and support made this unexpected time feel okay.

Paul had been pretty quiet, with the exception of his telling her that Gus had told him his story too. He'd told Paul that since she knew the whole thing it seemed right for him to know too. Plus, he wanted Paul to know that he intended to keep helping people that needed his kind of help, and he wanted Paul to point people in his direction. Clearly Gus had turned a corner, and that made Clare really happy.

Paul was happy about Gus, but he kept looking at her strangely. He said nothing about getting together later, or over the weekend. And she hadn't heard from him since.

Clare organized her day around finishing at least one cover letter and resume, just so she could tell Kate she'd accomplished something. But more and more she felt like what she was mailing wasn't right, like she was opening a door she really didn't want to go through.

It was before 5:00 when she got to Manna House, since she didn't live by the workday clock anymore. She found Paul in the kitchen making sure the pantry was stocked. He smiled when he saw her, a large smile, and then almost immediately the other look came into his eyes. The one she'd seen the week before. The one she couldn't identify.

"Hi Paul. How has your week been?" Clare started with small talk, but given the earliness of the hour, she had every intention of getting to the root of that look.

"Good. We've been busy, which I guess is a good thing. When I came I thought it was a bad thing when we were busy, because I thought it meant more people were on the street. Now I know that it just means they've heard about us, so they are getting dinner, instead of trying to figure out where the next meal comes from."

"That's good big picture thinking from the Director." She smiled, but he didn't.

"Paul – what's wrong? Something is obviously bothering you. I could tell last week, and I let it go, but now I see it again today. What's the matter?"

"You really want to know?"

"Yes."

"I'm thinking about leaving."

"What? Why would you do that? I thought you loved this job. What's changed?"

"Nothing about the job."

"Then what?"

"I just feel like it's wrong for me to have this job when you aren't working; if this had happened a few months ago, you would have applied and been a shoe-in."

"Oh my gosh. That's what you've been thinking? No, I don't deserve it more than you. You've done a great job. I know how to get the people served food and how to be welcoming to the guests, yes. But you've gotten donors lined up. And you've gotten new religious groups and volunteer organizations participating. You're getting people to see what's really going on with homeless people, in ways I never imagined." Clare stopped. "I guess when you first came, I kind of wondered why they needed someone like you, but I stopped wondering that a long time ago."

"Are you sure?"

"Yes. Let me tell you about what I have been thinking I want to do, although I'm not sure it's a reality."

As Clare told Paul her plan, he started to smile and nod, and then the smile got bigger, until finally she said, "Okay - now why are you looking like that?"

"Well, here's the thing. I think I have an idea for how you could fund yourself until your idea gets off the ground."

"Okay?" Clare had no idea what he was going to say next.

"I just applied for a grant, and there's a really good chance that we're going to get it. I wanted to surprise you, because it's really your idea."

"What are you talking about?"

"Well, remember when Gus was sick, and you gave Manna House as his address? And you thought about how hard it would be if you didn't have an address? Well, I applied for a grant to make this place into more of a center than just a meal place. The guests already think of it that way, so why not make it official? We'll serve as an address, an answering service, an e-mail. We'll put in a shower and laundry, so that people who are employable can get ready for an interview."

Clare could already envision it in her mind. "Wow. That's amazing. I love that idea."

"Here's the thing. I don't have the hours in the day to make this project happen. But I couldn't figure out how I was going to hire someone to implement it, and then work themselves out of a job."

She felt the excitement building in her, at what she thought he was about to say.

"What if you come on staff part-time for a year, and do the work to put this together? Assuming we get the grant, the money will be there, and in the meantime, you could build up your business. What do you think?"

"I love it! That would be so awesome. I mean, I know it's all a maybe, maybe you'll get the grant, maybe the board would let you hire me…"

"Oh, they already said it was up to me to find the person if we got the money. And like I said, I think it's a really good chance we'll get it – but technically - yes there is a maybe involved."

"There's one other thing." Clare said.

"What?" Paul asked.

"Is there any personnel policy against dating other staff members?" Clare could almost feel the voice in her head applauding. Finally, she had jumped into the unknown, saying out loud what was in her heart.

"No – it would have been pretty weird for them to make any policy like that when I was the only employee." He looked confused, and then the confusion cleared. He looked up at the clock. It was 5:20. He turned to Clare saying, "So, given the lack of policy, and if I didn't steal your job, and if you're not going to hate me forever for the times I was controlling and jealous in Immokalee, do you think you might be interested in giving us a try?"

The whole time they'd been talking, the space between them had been getting smaller. Paul reached out – and put his arms around her waist. His face was very close to hers now. He brushed a little of her hair away and touched her lips with his. First it was soft, then a little harder. And then it just was, and she wasn't thinking about anything anymore.

And then - there was a noise behind them. They turned to see that Gus was inside the room. "You guys left the front door unlocked. You want me to lock it for you?" Clare felt her face getting the embarrassing red color that made it clear to Gus that he'd seen what he thought he'd seen, even though they had quickly moved apart.

"Thanks Gus. Yeah that would be great – after all, the policy says doors locked until serving time. Don't want to confuse anybody by changing the system."

The crazier life got, the more people needed structure, and the guests of Manna House proved the rule.

Then Paul said, "But Gus, you don't have to go back out." Clare understood what Paul saying. Gus didn't feel like a guest anymore. He was a man with a mission now. A part of the Manna House care-giving team.

But Gus shook his head with a smile. "Nope, I'm going out. I belong on the other side of the door. I'm one of them. Always will be."

There was a time when hearing Gus say that would have made her sad. Now – it only felt true. Just like the truth that whatever came next in all of their lives, they had each found a home at Manna House.

# Acknowledgements

I want to thank the churches and ministries that have nurtured me on my faith journey as a child, pastor and writer over the years. Thank you to St. Paul's United Methodist Church, in Rochester Michigan, Princeton United Methodist Church, in Princeton, New Jersey, Basking Ridge Presbyterian Church, in Basking Ridge, New Jersey, Presbyterian Church of the Master, in Omaha, Nebraska, First Presbyterian Church of Sussex, in Sussex, New Jersey, Cedarkirk Presbyterian Camp and Conference Center, in Lithia, Florida, First Presbyterian Church of Brandon, in Brandon, Florida and Pleasantville Presbyterian Church, in Pleasantville, New York. I have learned so much from, and been so blessed to be part of, each of these communities.

Thank you to Rev. Barbara Brown Taylor and Dr. Rodger Nishioka. Their support and reading of my doctoral project, *Exploring Creative Writing as a Spiritual Practice*, were the impetus for beginning this project after the completion of my degree.

Many thanks to Jane Bullard and Gail Fortune for reading Finding Manna and giving me feedback that was incredibly helpful along the way. Thank you to Mark Orendorf for his help on the Florida ministries research. I'm grateful to have had the opportunity to learn about the life-changing work of Beth-El Farmworker Ministry, Guadalupe Center, and the Coalition of Immokalee Workers.

Most of all, I'm thankful to my family for their reading, editing skills, feedback, constant encouragement, support and love throughout the process of bringing this story to life.